Mary Kirby, Elizabeth Kirby

Beautiful birds in far-off lands

their haunts and homes

Mary Kirby, Elizabeth Kirby

Beautiful birds in far-off lands
their haunts and homes

ISBN/EAN: 9783337414344

Printed in Europe, USA, Canada, Australia, Japan

Cover: Foto ©Andreas Hilbeck / pixelio.de

More available books at **www.hansebooks.com**

BEAUTIFUL BIRDS

IN FAR-OFF LANDS:

THEIR HAUNTS AND HOMES.

BY

Mary and Elizabeth Kirby,

AUTHORS OF "THE WORLD AT HOME," "THE SEA AND ITS WONDERS," ETC.

———◆———

LONDON:

T. NELSON AND SONS, PATERNOSTER ROW;

EDINBURGH; AND NEW YORK.

1873.

Preface.

N the little volume now presented to the public, we have endeavoured to seek out the BEAUTIFUL BIRDS, to follow them to their native haunts, and to depict some of the scenes of their home life.

A mere description of the Birds would have failed to convey any idea of their loveliness; but the Coloured Illustrations which embellish the work bring them before our eyes with life-like reality.

These Beautiful Birds dwell in a land where winter never comes. Their gay plumage is suited to a climate which is as one long summer's day. The ruby, the emerald, the topaz, form a part of their toilette; but none of these gems can rival the sumptuousness of their attire.

In our own land, who amongst us would like to be without the Birds ?

It is true they are more soberly dressed, but do they not cheer our daily walks, and speak to us of gladness ?

Even in winter they do not altogether forsake us.

The Swift, and the Swallow, and the Painted Kingfisher have bidden us farewell ; but the friendly Robin is still at our side, and hops about our path, as though he had something to teach us.

And is it not this—To remind us of the goodness of the Creator in providing for the wants of every living thing ?

The little Birds have neither storehouse nor barn ; yet He feedeth them ; and not one of them falleth to the ground without His permission.

Contents.

CONTENTS.

BEAUTIFUL BIRDS.

I.

THE FOREST.

F you live in the country, I daresay you often go into the woods. And very pleasant it is there. You may find the blue-bell and the white anemone, and you may see the little squirrel sitting on the branches of the trees, or else leaping from bough to bough. You may think there are no woods so deep and shady as these. The grassy paths may seem like labyrinths ; and the stillness so profound, you may fancy, as the poet did, that the spirits of the wood wait and hold their peace while you pass by.

But in hot countries the woods are not like our woods. They are great dark forests, where the trees grow so thickly together, and are so tall, that if you looked up you could hardly see the sky. Then, there are a great many climbing-plants, that twist themselves round and round the trunks and branches of the trees. They are called vegetable cables, because they are so much like ropes, and they reach from one tree to another, and almost fill up the spaces between. The white man has to fight his way with his hatchet, or else burn himself a passage.

Dangers of every kind lurk in the forest. The quick subtle Indian dare not venture without his poisoned arrow, or the white man without the thunder and lightning of his gun. The venomous snake may lie coiled among the bushes, or traces of the savage jaguar be seen upon the path.

Birds, animals, and insects live undisturbed. It is their home; and on every side they are at work, hunting their prey, or escaping from danger. Man is not there to wage war upon them; but these wild creatures of the forest wage war upon each other, and the weak are always using some contrivance to protect themselves from the strong.

There are a great many curious things to be seen in the forest.

In the deepest gloom, where the trees shut out the sun, myriads of lights flit about, and twinkle like little stars. They flash here and there, and you might fancy that troops of fairies were carrying torches in their hands ; but there are no fairies in the case,—the lights are only the torches of the fire-flies that live in the recesses of the wood, and every night make a kind of illumination amongst the trees.

Then there are troops of monkeys, that run along the vegetable cables from one tree to the other, or swing from the branches by their tails, making a noise all the time as if they were talking to each other. When night comes they roll themselves into a ball, all huddled together as close as may be, to keep themselves warm. Sometimes it happens that a few little monkeys have not been alert enough to get into the ball, and are left shivering outside. They keep up a pitiful howling the whole night through, telling the rest how cold and miserable they are, and begging to be let in. But the others are very hard-hearted; they pay no attention, and go quietly off to sleep.

In Tropical America vast rivers run through the forest, and numberless streams and creeks wind along, twisting and doubling in every direction. On the bank is a complete wall of forest, that presents a firm, dense barrier. Now and then a sad story has reached us of travellers lost in the forest, and who have tried to make their way by the side of the stream. But the thick brushwood and jungle, that grew close to the water's edge, has stopped their progress, and made it impossible to push on further.

Even the fierce jaguar, the tiger of the forest, often loses himself in the tangled maze. He cannot force his way, supple as he is, through the labyrinth. He is obliged to climb a tree, and travel for miles along the branches, passing from one tree to another, and running up and down the vegetable ropes and ladders with the adroitness of a monkey.

While he remains in this leafy home, the poor monkeys form his chief supply of food. They flee before him with shrill screams, and use all their nimbleness to get out of his way.

The wall of forest presents a wonderful spectacle. Often it is gloomy and dark, and the trees are of a uniform colour. But here and there a mighty tree has pushed its way up through the mass, as if resolved to get more light and air. Its splendid crown of flowers, red, white, or yellow, towers aloft.

Here are the palms in full magnificence— crowned in the season with beauty. And, now and then, the scene is like fairyland.

Brilliant blossoms of white and scarlet over-hang the water, and flowering creepers hang around the trees, and droop from the branches like festoons. Here, in the more open spots where the wall of forest recedes, are found the Beautiful Birds we are about to describe. It is their home and dwelling.

Flocks of Parrots glisten in the sun, clad in glowing scarlet, or green, or gold. Humming-birds, like gems of beauty, come to seek honey and insects from the forest flowers. Fly-catchers gleam and sparkle. Water-fowl of snowy plumage sport on the streams, and their white dresses contrast with those of the red Flamingo, or the scarlet Ibis, that stand patiently fishing on the shore.

Here and there a black object appears on the water, that looks like a log of wood floating slowly down. But it is nothing of the kind. It is the fierce alligator watching for his prey. And here, too, fringing many an islet in the river, is seen the wonderful mangrove, a tree that can grow on the shores of the ocean, with its roots bathed by the salt waves.

A belt of mangroves fringing the river-bank will push itself farther and farther, until a portion of land will actually be reclaimed and wrested, as it were, from the water.

The mangrove has a curious way of lifting itself out of the ground or swamp. Its roots form a number of arches, which rise up to some height and spread themselves far and wide. From the midst of the arches springs the stem, clothed with branches and gay with flowers.

All among the arches, and in the damp black mud out of which they spring, millions of insects, and crabs, and living creatures sport in safety.

Man cannot approach them, for the air is fatal to him, though harmless to them.

There is a special provision made by Nature for the mangrove. The seed drops, at the proper season, and is in danger of being carried away, by the stream, from the muddy bank on which alone it could grow. But it is possessed of a small rootlet, by which it can attach itself at once to the swampy ground, and remain there in security. These rootlets are put forth, and the stem gradually rises up from the midst, and another mangrove is added to the great belt of trees that lines the bank.

At times the mighty river becomes swollen by the rains. Then, huge waves rise and march rapidly onward. It overflows its banks, and rushes through the forest with a terrible roar and crash.

The forest trees, gigantic as they are, become uprooted, and are carried away by the stream as though they were reeds or rushes. The monkeys, the jaguars, all the creatures of the forest are swept away. And the gloomy alligator swims where lately they made their home in the branches.

WHERE TO FIND THE BIRDS OF PARADISE.

F you turn to the map of Asia, you will find a number of islands lying to the south of Malacca, and forming a link between Asia and Australia.

These islands are in the very midst of the Tropics. The warm Tropical seas bathe their coasts, and dark dense forests cover many of them from the sea-shore to the top of the highest mountain.

Beautiful birds, and insects of wondrous size and rainbow hues, flit among the deep recesses, almost like creatures of another world. The white man rarely visits this far-off land. The dangers that he would meet with are too great. The natives, in many places, are fierce and cunning, and would kill him with their spears or weapons; and yet without their aid he could not make his way through the forest depths, let him try as he might.

Do you see the great island of New Guinea? It is one of the largest islands in the world. The traveller might sail round its shores for weeks, and fancy he had reached a continent. A portion of the island is yet unknown, and no white man has set his foot there.

The people who inhabit New Guinea are called Papuans. Their skin is black, but has not the deep jet of the Negro. Their hair is very peculiar, and the fashion in which they wear it is just as curious.

When the Papuan is young, his hair grows in little tufts or curls all over his head, and is very dry and frizzly. By degrees it becomes a kind of frizzly mop, and when it has reached this state it is considered to be the height of fashion.

The Papuan takes the utmost pains with his

mop-like hair, and tries hard to prevent its getting tangled.   He keeps a comb made of bamboo,
with long teeth like the prongs of a fork, always
ready for use.   And if he has a few minutes to
spare, he busies himself in combing his frizzly
locks.   His house is quite a curiosity, but we
should not like to live in it.

In some of the villages by the sea-coast, the
houses stand in the water ; and you must go to
them by means of a bridge.   The roof is like a
boat turned wrong side upwards ; and the house
itself stands on poles to raise it above the water.

Should you like to know a little more. about
these strange-looking houses ?   The floor is very
uneven, and often has great holes in it.   It is
made of rubbish—such as sticks and leaves and
old boards—put rudely together.   You can
hardly walk over this rough floor ; and a child
might easily slip through one of the holes.

The very poles on which the house rests often
lean as if they would fall ; and, worse than this, if
you looked up, you would see a row of human
skulls hanging under the eaves.   They are the

skulls of men of another tribe, whom the Papuan has killed in battle.

New Guinea is a very interesting place to the naturalist. Here are many curious insects, such as are found nowhere else. And here, and in the islands close by, called the Aru Islands, are found the Birds of Paradise. They live nowhere else.

The eager naturalist who wishes to possess them, or to see them in their native haunts, must track them to this far-off land; but the dangers and trials of such a journey are very great. It was not till within the last few years that the way was opened by an enterprising traveller, * who went on a voyage of discovery. He came to this very spot, to obtain specimens of the Birds of Paradise, and to study their habits. If we follow in his steps, we shall behold many curious scenes, and visit places hitherto unknown.

* A. R. Wallace, Esq.

III.

A SCENE IN THE FOREST.

'T is early morning, and as yet the sun has not smitten the earth with his scorching beams. The forest is alive with brilliant creatures, that, a few hours hence, will be hidden in its coolest and deepest recesses.

The Parrots, and the Pigeons, and the gorgeous little Fly-catchers, glisten among the branches, and are full of animation. But the scene I am about to describe does not relate to these.

Do you notice yonder tree, with great spreading boughs that grow from the top of the stem, and form a kind of leafy plateau? At present the plateau is clear of occupants. But, creeping silently towards the tree, you may see a native with his bow and arrow. Look more narrowly, and you will perceive a hut woven of the branches, and quite hidden amongst them. It is so carefully concealed that not even a bird can guess it is there.

The native climbs the tree and creeps into the bower, for such it may be called. He lies there, silent and motionless, and the forest sights and sounds go on around him.

Presently a bird alights on the green plateau over his head. I can scarce give you, by mere words, any idea of its surpassing beauty.

Its head and neck are of a delicate yellow, and have the effect of velvet. Its throat is of an emerald green, and there are deep green plumes across the forehead.

But the principal ornament by which it is distinguished is a plume of long, delicate feathers of an orange gold colour. By this plume you see at once that you have before you the most lovely inhabitant of the Tropics—the great Bird of Paradise. The native sees the bird as well. He

bends his bow and fixes his arrow, but he still
remains motionless. The time for action has not
yet arrived. In an instant, another Bird of Paradise alights on the tree. Then a third;—the birds
are gathering fast upon the leafy plateau. They
are full of activity, and fly from branch to branch,
and wave their plumes until the tree seems alive
with them. The effect is wonderful, and cannot
be surpassed even in this land of beauty.

Sometimes, a bird will crouch down as if in
frolic, and raise its plumes over its head till they
look like fans of shining gold.

But all the time it is thus in the enjoyment of
its life and vigour, an enemy is on the watch.
The eye of the native is keenly fixed upon it.
Another moment, and an arrow with a blunted
point strikes its lovely head or breast.

The poor bird is stunned, and drops down,—its
forest joys ended. As it lies helpless on the
ground, a boy, who is waiting for the purpose,
picks it up and kills it without injuring its plumage.

The blow has come so silently and unexpectedly

that the rest of the birds do not seem to know what has happened. They continue their merry game, until another falls, and then another.

At length, it occurs to them that some enemy is near, and their only safety is in flight. Then the Indian knows his morning's work is over. He quits his lurking-place, picks up his dead birds, and carries them home.

IV.

PREPARING THE BIRDS FOR SALE.

WHEN the native has reached his home, he sets to work to prepare the Birds of Paradise for sale. He intends to dispose of them to the traders who come that way, or to any Europeans who may chance to land. He cuts off the wings and feet, and removes the skin. Then he puts a stick through the body, wraps it in a palm-leaf, and dries it in the smoke. By this process the body itself is shrunk almost to nothing; but the flowing plumes retain their beauty. These, indeed, are all the native bird-stuffer cares about.

Some of the smoke-dried specimens, such as I

have been describing, used to be brought to
Europe.   No one had the least idea what birds
they were, or from what country they came.
They were supposed to have no legs, and all kinds
of foolish tales were told about them.   They were
said never to touch the ground, but to live on
dew.   Indeed, the name of "Bird of Paradise"
was given them on this account; a name they
have retained ever since.

By degrees the truth came to light.   It was
found out that the Bird of Paradise was possessed
of legs, and could settle on the ground, and feed
like other birds.   In fact, there was nothing
supernatural about it.

The chiefs of New Guinea, and of the other
islands, trade in the Birds of Paradise, and take
care to keep the trade in their own hands.   They
do not like a stranger to interfere with it; indeed,
both they and their subjects dislike the coming of
the white man, and throw many obstacles in his
way; added to which, in some of the islands there
is scarcely any food.   The natives are too lazy to
work, and would almost rather starve.   Yet the

soil would produce an hundredfold, if they would take the pains to cultivate it.

This is especially the case in the places where the sago-palm grows; for sago and fish are all the native seems to care for.

The tree is something like the cocoa-nut palm, but its stem is thicker, and it has great prickly leaves that cover the trunk. These leaves are fifteen feet long, and immensely thick. But in spite of their thickness they are very light, and can easily be carried. The people make great use of these giant leaves. They build houses of them, thatch with them, and floor with them. Nothing can be more convenient.

As for the trunk, it feeds millions of people. At the proper season it is cut down, the leaves taken away, and a slit made from one end to the other. Then the natives come with wooden clubs and break the pith, and clear it out. It is carried away in baskets to a washing-machine, which stands in the river, and is made of the palm-wood itself. When the pith or sago is ready, the women employ themselves in making it into

bread.   The bread is baked in a curious little
oven, with divisions in it.   The sago is poured in,
and fills the spaces between the divisions.   It is
baked in five minutes into nice hot cakes, which
are very delicate when eaten fresh.   But they are
most useful dried, and put by as a supply of food.
It is true they get as hard as wood, but the
people like them, and are accustomed to live almost entirely upon them.   Little children may be
seen gnawing the sago-cakes, as our English children gnaw a crust of bread.

The European cannot thrive on such a diet;
and it requires all his love for science to enable
him to exist.   Only one European has ever made
a lengthened stay there; and he was the enterprising naturalist who endured every hardship,
and even risked his life, to obtain a thorough
knowledge of the Birds of Paradise.

V

THE RED BIRD OF PARADISE.

ATURE has not given to the Bird of Paradise any musical powers. His voice is curious, but not at all harmonious. Early in the morning, a loud, harsh note is heard to resound through the forest, as though some one were crying out "Wok!" "wok!" It is the morning cry of the Great Bird of Paradise, as he wakes up to seek his breakfast from the trees.

It is a signal for the forest cries to begin, and soon a chorus sounds from branch and bush. Parrots chatter and scream. All kinds of birds chirp or whistle, or utter their morning notes, until the noise is almost deafening.

The Bird of Paradise, with his golden plumage, has many relations. Some of these have never been beheld by Europeans. For ages, successive generations of them have sported in the depths of the forest, and gladdened no human eye.

The bird in the picture has plumes of a rich crimson, tipped with white, and more gorgeous than you can imagine. His throat is of a rich green, and he has a little tuft of green feathers on his forehead. The most curious ornaments he possesses are two long, stiff quills, something like whalebone, that hang down with a graceful curve. When the poor bird is dead and lies upon his back, these quills form themselves into a circle and meet at his neck.

The hen-bird does not possess the gay colours or the flowing plumes of her mate. She is a plain-looking bird, and does not attract any attention. Nor did the various charms of the male bird appear at once. When he was young, his long quills were mere short feathers, and gave no promise of what they would afterwards become. And it was only by degrees that the lovely quills and wonderful plumes made their appearance.

The Red Birds of Paradise are only found in one spot. They live in a small island close by New Guinea. This is one of the islands where the traveller finds little comfort and scarcely anything to eat.

The natives pay every year a tribute of Birds of Paradise to a neighbouring chief. But they will not take any further trouble. They neither plant nor sow. Each native has, if he can, a frizzly-headed Papuan for a slave, and lives himself in perfect idleness.

Even though the cocoa-nut palm grows in the island, it does not enrich the people. They do not cultivate any vegetables, but they cut down the green cocoa-nuts, and eat them instead.

In the forests of this island the Red Birds of Paradise have their home. They are not shot with a blunt arrow, but another mode of catching them is employed.

There is a great climbing-plant that grows in the forest and bears a red seed. The bird is very

fond of the seed, and when it is ripe comes to eat
it. The hunter knows this; so he gathers the
bunch of seed and fastens it to a stick. He has
a long piece of cord with him, and thus provided,
he walks off into the forest.

He soon finds a tree on which the birds are
likely to come and perch, and he climbs it with
the agility of a monkey. Then he ties his bunch
of seed to a branch, making it look as if it grew
there, and leaving a noose to dangle in such a way
that the poor bird is almost sure to get caught in it.

When all is ready, he gets down and sits under
the tree, holding the end of the cord in his hand.
Sometimes he has to wait a whole day, or even
longer, before a bird will come. But he has
great patience, and nothing else to do.

Presently a bird will come and perch on the
bough where the ripe seed is displayed. It looks
very tempting, and the poor silly bird goes to it,
and begins to peck at the bait. Its legs soon get
entangled in the cord ; and then the hunter gives
it a pull, and down comes the poor bird, and is
caught.

An attempt was made * to keep the Birds of Paradise alive in a cage. They were very lively at first—for it is their nature to be in constant motion—and they ate fruit and insects, or whatever food was given them. But it was soon seen that captivity was fatal to these children of the forest. At the end of a few days, they fell off the perch and died.

* By Mr. Wallace.

VI.

THE KING BIRD OF PARADISE.

LOSE by New Guinea, at a little distance to the south, lie a group of islands called the Aru Islands. We seem here to have left the civilized world behind; and we should not have ventured to so remote a spot but for the beautiful birds we shall find in its deep, dark forests,—forests not yet explored, and with scarce any of their treasures brought to light.

What is that lovely creature which is flying from branch to branch? The place where we stand is not the dense part of the forest. The trees here are a moderate size, and the ground is more open. The bird is devouring the fruit of the tree on which it is perched. It flutters its wings and makes a curious sound, something like the whirring noise of a wheel. And, like the rest of its tribe, it is always in motion; you never see it still an instant.

Let us admire, for a few moments, its surpassing beauty. Its body is about the size of our English Thrush, but how different a costume has Nature given to it! You can see in the Picture how the bird is dressed. The white plumage underneath the body is soft and glossy as silk. And between the rich purple of the throat and the white of the body is a band or stripe of the most brilliant green.

But these exquisite colours are only part of the ornaments that Nature has bestowed. Do you see those two fan-like appendages on either side the body and beneath the wings? They are tipped with the richest green,—and can be spread out when the bird chooses. In the Picture it has done so, and you see them to perfection.

Then you must notice the long tail-wires, as they are called, which hang down, and are tipped

with two green feathers or buttons. These
wonderful buttons are not found in any other
species. They belong only to the King Bird of
Paradise,—and it is a King Bird that we see
before us.

The naturalist, gazing for the first time on this
gem of beauty, is filled with delight. But the
natives smile at his expressions of admiration.
After all, what is it but a mere "Goby-goby," as
they call it,—a bird as common with them as the
Thrush or the Robin is with us! They see nothing
to wonder at ; still less to come thousands of miles
to obtain !

And it is a great mystery to them why the
naturalist should fill his hut with all those stuffed
birds, and insects ; and butterflies as large as your
hand, and dressed in green and gold and crimson.
Large and splendid as they are, nothing can be
more common. And surely the people who live
in his country, and make knives and looking-
glasses, and all manner of wonderful things,
cannot care about butterflies and goby-gobies !

One day an old man made a guess on the

subject that amused the naturalist,* and caused him
to laugh.

The old man declared he had found out the
secret. No doubt the birds, and all the stuffed
creatures, that the white man was going to carry
away in his box, would come to life when they
reached his country! Yes, that must be the
reason!

At one time of the year, the birds are very
merry indeed. They hold what the natives call
their dancing-parties. Do you remember the tree
I spoke of, with its broad green top like a plateau?
At a certain season, and when the birds are in
full plumage, they come here in parties of twenty
or more, and begin to play about, or, as the natives
say, to dance. They put themselves in all kinds
of attitudes, and wave their plumes about till the
tree seems alive. This is the time the most
favourable for the naturalist: he can now behold
the birds in their full beauty. At other seasons
they moult, and lose their feathers, as other birds
do, and are not worth preserving.

* Mr. Wallace.

THE VISIT OF THE TRADERS TO THE
ARU ISLANDS.

———◆◆———

CANNOT quit these far-off islands without giving you a little more information concerning them.

We are, as I said before, out of the track of civilized life. Vessels rarely find their way hither. The people are mere savages; there are neither towns nor cities, such as we are accustomed to see; and the dense Tropical forest stretches for miles around us. But Nature revels in undisturbed freedom; and creatures of beauty and plants of wild and splendid luxuriance are found on every hand. The group called the Aru

Islands consists of one large island and a number of smaller ones which surround it. The sea that bathes the shore is shallow and full of coral. And the pearl-oyster is found here, and forms part of the trade of the natives.

When I speak of trade and traders, you must not think of white people. The traders are a motley group that come from the neighbouring islands, or from China and Malacca. They come in native boats called proas, and bring all kinds of merchandise,—such as knives and tobacco, and even fancy goods, such as looking-glasses and crockery. And in return, they take away Birds of Paradise and sugar-canes, and the few commodities afforded by the country.

I must tell you that the sugar-cane grows here abundantly, and the sailors who come in the boats are very fond of it. They eat it greedily, and are constantly chewing and sucking it, and cutting at it with their knives. They never seem as if they could get enough.

The place where the traders meet is on the beach, and has a row of sheds, called, by the

natives, houses. Part of the shed is used by the
trader, when he comes, as a store in which to put
his merchandise ; and during his stay, a little
bustle goes on in the desolate spot.

All behind the village is the dense forest,
with its swarms of living creatures; its Birds
of Paradise, its gigantic butterflies, and its spin-
ning spiders, that spread a net as thick as a
veil, and strong enough to entangle you. Sometimes you come on the spider itself, a great
yellow creature of monstrous size, and covered
with spots.

The beach, in some places, presents a wonderful
appearance. Mighty branches droop down from
the trees and are clothed with fantastic flowers.
These flowers do not belong to the tree. They are
of the Orchis tribe, and have inserted themselves
into the branch, and seem to spring from it.
Others, of strange and brilliant form, hang down
by threads, and look as if they grew in the air.
And here and there, a palm raises its graceful
crown, or a tree-fern appears in all its beauty,
and mounts up to the height of thirty feet. The

Aru people are not industrious, but they grow some kinds of vegetables, such as yams and plantains. They are very fond of shell-fish, and consume quantities of cockles.

Their most fatal propensity is that of drinking a spirituous liquor called arrack. The traders bring the arrack in boxes, each box containing a number of bottles. The Aru man can easily buy the box. He has only to go out fishing, and get a quantity of trepang. The trepang is a sea-slug, and crawls at the bottom of the sea. It is a disagreeable-looking creature, but the Chinese have a great fancy for it, and cook and eat it as a delicacy.

The native goes out in a boat, and dives down into the water and picks it up. He dries and prepares it in his hut—a process easily managed—and gets it ready for the market. And then he can cut ratan, which is a climbing, reed-like palm that grows in the forest. It has long slender stems, armed at every joint with spines, and can run as well as climb.

Sometimes the stems run along the ground to

an immense distance, or they climb up some lofty palm, and embrace it so closely that it dies. Then the curious twisted arms of the ratan are left like so many snakes, turning and twisting and holding each other up. The tree has decayed and gone, and the ratan stems look as though they were embracing the air.

The dense thickets in the forest are made up a good deal of this creeping, climbing palm. The naturalist who wants to force a way through it, is caught and hooked by the spines, and must have his path cleared with a hatchet. But though so troublesome to the traveller, and, as far as he is concerned, the scourge of the forest, the ratan can be turned to good account. The natives plat it into mats and baskets, and twist it into ropes and cordage. So strong are these natural ropes—the cordage, we might term it, of the forest—that in some parts of the Tropics bridges are made of them across the rivers and streams.

With the trepang and the ratan together the native can buy plenty of arrack ; and it is so much the worse for him. He carries it home, calls his family and friends together, and they have a regular drinking-bout.

His carouse often ends in a very sad way, for the men get so excited, they seem as if they were going mad. They will tear and break all that comes in their way.

VIII.

BIRDS THAT NO WHITE MAN HAS SEEN.

———— ✦ ————

OU must not suppose that the beautiful birds you have seen in the Pictures include the whole family of the Birds of Paradise. This is far from being the case. Many birds, of most lovely and exquisite plumage, flit about in remote and secluded spots, and have never been beheld by the white man. He can only judge of their appearance by the few smoke-dried specimens that are procured from the natives, and which give but a slight idea of the splendour of the living birds. Still, we are glad to know that such rare and beautiful creatures do actually exist, and to glean every particular concerning them.

There is the Magnificent Bird of Paradise; and well does it deserve the title. It is very rare, and is only found in New Guinea and in one other island. It has a mass of feathers, of a yellow colour, on its neck, which form themselves into a kind of hood or mantle. Its tail-wires are of a rich blue, and form themselves into a circle. In another species, if possible more gorgeously attired, the mantle or hood is yellow, and the breast green. The skin on the head is bare; but is of a rich blue, with bands of black. Then there is the rarest of the whole family, the Superb Bird of Paradise. We only know it by an occasional smoke-dried specimen, that has come under the notice of the white man. It lives in the central part of New Guinea, beyond his reach or sight, and is very difficult to procure. The natives do not care to take the trouble, and value the bird very slightly. They call it the Black Bird of Paradise, and give no information about its habits. Then there is a bird which has a num-

ber of shaft-like feathers springing from its head.
Its breast is a brilliant yellow, which changes into
green and blue every minute. The band of
feathers on the back of the head shine and sparkle
like precious stones; and over the forehead is a
patch of white that shines like satin. The six
feathers or shafts are the most wonderful part of
its appearance, and when alive it must baffle
description. But it is rarely seen, and its dry
and shrunk skin is all the European can obtain.

I must not omit to mention an entirely new
specimen, found by Mr. Wallace himself, and
named after him. It is called Standard Wing;
and besides the usual gorgeous colours in which it
is dressed, it has a pair of long feathers springing
from the wings, and which are in no other species.
The bird is met with in the Spice Islands, and
clings to the branch of the tree as the Woodpecker
does. It has a harsh creaking note, like the creak
of a gate. The long feathers, I should tell you,
are of a white colour, and can be raised or lowered
at pleasure. From them, the bird has its name
of Standard Wing.

The birds I have mentioned belong to one tribe of the Paradise order ; but they have some relations with long bills, and that are called Long-billed Birds of Paradise.

There is a magnificent bird of this class, with a long curved bill, and that is called the Twelve-wired Bird, because of the twelve wires or shafts that spring from under its wings, and curve in a fantastic manner. It flies about among the flowers, extracting sugar from them, for sugar is its favourite food. It loves to hover about the sago-palm, when the great spike of flowers is about to unclose. It has large, strong feet, with which it can clasp the spathe of the flower, while it feasts on the rich contents. But it has all the restlessness of its family ; and when it has sucked a little juice, it soon flies off to another tree in quest of more.

Its loud shrill call may be heard a long way off. It begins high, and gradually sinks lower and lower, till it reaches the last note, and then the bird darts away.

The natives hunt the Twelve-wired Bird, and lay

a snare for it.   They find out the tree on which it
roosts, and which is more of a bush than a tree.
They climb up in the night, and shoot the poor
bird with one of their blunt arrows ; or they
throw a piece of cloth over it and take it alive.
Then there is the Long-tailed Bird of Paradise,
which has also a slender bill, and a tail a little
like a Peacock.   It has also a number of plumes
on each side of the breast, that stand up, and are
striped with the most brilliant green and blue.
No European has ever seen it alive.   It lives
in the unknown parts of New Guinea, where the
inhabitants are so uncivilized that it is not safe
to venture near them.

It is said that the nest of the bird is under-
ground, and that it has two holes,—one for an
entrance and the other for an outlet.   This is
what the natives report, and they are generally
pretty correct.

I might weary you with descriptions of these
beautiful birds, and yet you can form very little
idea of how they appear in their native forests.
They are so difficult to obtain that the naturalist

could only procure a few specimens during a residence of many months on the islands.

An attempt was made to penetrate into the unknown districts of New Guinea, in order to find some of the species I have named, and which have never been seen alive by the white man. But the dangers were very great. The natives of the coast declared that the people of the interior would kill any stranger who made his appearance amongst them. And when the naturalist* did arrive at a place where some of the birds were said to be found, he had not a single guide or interpreter. He remained there a month without being able to understand a word that was said, and had to make signs for what he wanted.

Nor did he succeed in his purpose. The birds were still many miles distant, and he found it impossible to penetrate further into such a barbarous and inaccessible country.

But in these very districts, remote and peopled with savages, has Nature stored up her choicest productions. They are not accessible to any but

* Mr. Allen.

the natives. The rocks, mountains, swamps, and the dense wall of forest, shut them up from the rest of the world. Now and then a specimen reaches us of surpassing loveliness, and we gaze with wonder and delight. But the shrunk body and smoke-dried skin is very different from the living, moving creature, radiant with beauty, and flashing light as it were from its wings !

IX

THE BLUE-HEADED TANAGER.

HERE is a tribe of birds very familiar to us all; they belong to a large, well-marked division, in the great family of birds, called Perchers and Climbers. They are seen hopping and perching and climbing everywhere, and they are known by the name of Finches.

The poor little Finch is often persecuted by the farmer with much injustice. It is found amongst the corn, and the owner of the field, seeing it very busy, thinks it is making havoc of the grain. But in reality the Finch is doing nothing of the kind. It is picking out the seeds from some tall, troublesome weeds that grow among the wheat.

If the little Finches were let alone, they would devour an immense quantity of these seeds, and prevent the weed from spreading. .

There are a vast number of the Finch tribe in England, and you know them well. There is the Goldfinch, the Bullfinch, the Chaffinch, and many more. It has been said that the number of weeds they keep under would cover many thousand acres.

How important it is to know our friends from our foes, and to spare the little birds !

I should not have introduced the Finch to your notice, but that he has a relation in these Tropical countries of which we are speaking.

Here he is in the Picture, and you can perceive how much more gaily he is dressed than our humble birds at home. His colours are brilliant. He wears green, and red, and blue ; and his plumage looks like velvet. He is a very familiar bird in the Tropics, and fills the same place that the Sparrow does at home. He is to be seen everywhere, glittering and flashing among the trees in the garden or orchard. He is not afraid of anything, but hops, and perches, and chirps, and is quite at his ease. He is not called the Finch. He has another name in this part of the world. He is the Tanager. There is a brilliant little bird, called the Scarlet Tanager, that is found in the forests of North America, and that has a glowing band of red on his wings. He is a very sociable bird, and ventures near the abode of man. He will come to the gardens to seek for fruit and insects, and will even place his nest on a tree by the roadside. But as soon as the young Tanagers are old enough, the parent birds will lead them away southward to escape the winter.

The old birds choose the night as the safest time for flitting, and glide through the woods followed by their little ones. Many families may be seen travelling in this way, on their route to a warmer spot.

The love of the parent birds for their young is very touching. Nothing will induce them to forsake their offspring. I can relate a little story to prove the fact.

A naturalist, who was very fond of studying the habits of birds, once caught a young Tanager, and carried it to his home. He then procured a cage, placed his prisoner within it, and hung the cage in a tree. There was a nest in the tree occupied by a number of young birds called Orioles. The parent Orioles kept flying backwards and forwards to feed their brood, and the naturalist hoped they would take pity on the little Tanager in the cage, and give it something to eat. But no such thing seemed likely to happen. The parent Orioles were far too busy attending to the wants of their own offspring to notice the Tanager, though they flew close by it. And as the poor little captive refused to be fed by the naturalist, there was some danger lest it should die of starvation.

Such a fate would, indeed, have befallen it, but that a deliverer was at hand. A Scarlet Tanager, full-grown, and no doubt the parent bird come in search of its little one, arrived at the cage, and made an attempt to get in. This it could not do, and after many fruitless efforts it flew away. But

very soon it returned, carrying an insect in its
bill, which it offered to the captive. This time
the hungry little Tanager did not refuse to be fed,
and the parent bird continued to bring insects and
other food until night. Then it took up its abode
in the tree close by the cage. The Orioles seemed
offended at the intrusion, and treated it with the
utmost insolence. But the Tanager bore their
insults with patience, and seemed resolved that
nothing should drive it to forsake its charge.
Some time passed, and the young Tanager grew
larger and stronger, and quite able to fly. The
parent bird did all it could to coax the prisoner
out of the cage, and made use of every note and
gesture, as it appeared, of entreaty and persuasion.
But the bars of the cage presented an obstacle
not to be removed, and the poor birds were both
of them in despair.

At length the owner of the garden, who had
watched all this with great interest, felt his heart
relent. He placed a ladder against the tree, and
climbing up to the cage, opened the door. The
scene that followed repaid his kindness and

humanity.   Out came the Tanager, and was
received by the parent bird with cries of delight.
Then both together, and still uttering notes of
rapture, they took the way to the forest.

X.

THE SUMMER RED BIRD.

HERE is another species of Tanager that is found in North America, and that I must not pass over. He is called the Summer Red Bird, and is of a rich vermilion colour, with legs and feet of a light blue. He is solitary in his habits, and likes to haunt that part of the forest which is filled with stunted shrubs and trees. But he is careful to keep to the warm districts, and cannot endure the slightest cold. At the least approach of it, he takes his departure, and is, literally, a bird of the summer.

When the Tanagers move from one part of the country to another, they rise high in the air, and

fly by day, instead of during the darkness of night.
When night comes they dive into the woods, as
if to roost; and their peculiar note may be heard
very plainly. The female bird seems to be re-
peating the words "Chicky, chucky," over and
over again. But her partner has a loud and rather
agreeable whistle, like a shake on some musical
instrument.

The female bird is seldom seen; and her plain
costume is hardly to be distinguished from the
foliage amid which she hides herself. But the
brilliant plumage of her mate flashes and glances
hither and thither as he moves about, and renders
him an object of the greatest beauty. He is indeed of the number of beautiful birds!

The nest of the Summer Red Bird is fixed on
some forked branch of a tree. The birds choose
often a tree on the open road, or in some part of
the wood that has been cleared. The nest is made
in rather a slovenly manner, of dried stalks and
weeds. It is so loosely fixed that a sharp blow
may shake it off. The eggs are of a light blue
colour, and the parent birds sit upon them by

turns, and evince the greatest anxiety for their safety.

The Summer Red Bird feeds on insects, and seems to prefer those of the beetle tribe. He will swallow very large ones indeed, such as you would hardly suppose possible. And he likes to pursue his prey on the wing, as the Fly-catchers do.

These beautiful birds are often seen perched on the branches of a vine that grows wild in that country, and is called the muscadine. In England we cultivate the grape in hot-houses, with the utmost care. But in the warm parts of America it may be seen everywhere.

Sometimes the vine climbs up the stem of some lofty tree, and turns round and round the branches until it reaches the extremities, when it still goes on growing, and appears to swing in the air. Rich clusters of grapes hang in profusion; and when they are ripe a shake will bring them down.

The traveller, coming that way, welcomes the sight of the fruitful vine, and stops to refresh himself with its abundance.

XI

THE PARROT.

———◆———

THERE is a tribe of birds, in the forest, better known to us and more familiar than the Birds of Paradise. Many of them find their way to England, not as dead and smoke-dried specimens, but as creatures of living beauty. I mean the family of Parrots. In England we see them shut up in cages; but in their native forests their splendid dresses shine and sparkle among the trees, until the branches seem alive with blue, and scarlet, and emerald.

The Parrot has been said to resemble its lively neighbour, the Monkey. You rarely if ever see it attempt to walk. Like the monkey, it climbs

nimbly from bough to bough, and swings itself
about, hanging by its bill and claws. These useful members serve it both for hands and for feet.

As it climbs from bough to bough, the tender
green twigs around are a kind of meadow or pasture in which it delights. It will cling by its
bill to the bough overhead. Then, with one of
its feet, it grasps a branch by its side, and with
the other foot it takes hold of a twig on the
other side. Thus it makes its way through the
trees as fast as it can.

The naturalist, who has carefully studied the
subject, can tell by looking at the bill what kind
of food the bird subsists upon. And the bill of
the Parrot tells its own story. It is intended to
do hard work, and to crack the forest nuts, and
get out the kernels. It has, therefore, a peculiar
form, and it would be worth our while to pause
a moment, and look at it.

It is a strong, sharp, hooked instrument, which
the Parrot can drive into the hardest shell, and
make a hole in it. And it is worked by very
powerful muscles indeed. The Parrot's large, full

cheek is taken up with these great muscles. They work both jaws—the upper as well as the lower. The Parrot's upper jaw is not fixed, as ours is. It never snaps its bill; but it can work its jaws together, and in a way in which we cannot. This is why the Parrot's bill is so amazingly strong.

If you could see some of the forest nuts that it cracks, you would understand the reason of this great provision of strength.

The shell of the fruit is as hard as iron, but the Parrot can wrench it open with its bill, or drive a hole in it. While it does so, it holds the fruit in its foot, as in a hand, and puts it in the right position with its great fleshy tongue.

What with its strong foot, its powerful bill, and its jaws, the Parrot is amply provided for by Nature, and able to maintain itself in plenty.

Perhaps you would like to know how the Parrots spend the day when they are at home in their native forests.

Very early in the morning they rouse themselves from sleep, and begin to chatter, and scream, and make a great noise. Then they all fly into the sunshine, and settling on the top of a tree, begin to dress their plumage, which is rather damp with the dews of night. They next look about for their breakfasts; and this is generally the wild-cherry, or some other fruit. They break the stones with their strong bills, and pick out the kernels and eat them. Then they go in quest of clear water to bathe in; and this they seem to enjoy very much indeed. They roll over and over, and play about like children on the edge of the pool, and dip their heads and wings into the water, so as to scatter it all over their plumage. By this time the sun is getting hot, and they retire to the deep recesses of the forest, where it is always cool and shady. They give over screaming and chattering, and settle themselves on the boughs for a nap. And then the silence is so deep you might hear a leaf drop to the ground, although the trees overhead are crowded with Parrots.

But the stillness only lasts through the noontide heat. In the evening the Parrots wake up,

and make as much noise as ever. They sup, as
they breakfasted, upon the kernels of the fruits,
and then go to the water to bathe. Again follows
the business of dressing and pluming their feathers, and after this they go to rest. But they do
not roost in the branches where they took their
afternoon's nap. Their sleeping-room is a hollow
tree, scooped out by the Woodpecker. As many
Parrots get in as the hollow will contain, and the
rest hook themselves to the bark by their claws
and bills, and hang there through the night.

The Parrot lays her eggs in these hollow trees.
She does not make a nest, but lays them on the
rotten wood ; and the whole flock lay their eggs
together in the same tree.

XII.

MORE ABOUT THE PARROT.

HERE is a gift possessed by the Parrot which makes his society very amusing. You will guess what I mean. He has the power of articulating words; in fact, he may be taught to speak.

The Parrots do not all possess this faculty. There is a splendid American Parrot that cannot be taught to say anything. But a relation of his, who is dressed in simple gray, can chatter away famously if he meets with any one to teach him. He will even appear as if taking the utmost pains to learn. He listens to his teacher, and repeats the sentences over and over until he is perfect, and can say them correctly. He will even talk in his sleep.

This power of imitation in the bird is very curious, if we take the trouble to think about it. His abode is far away from man, and it is only by chance that the faculty is awakened. But there it is, ready to develop itself at any moment.

The Indians make a trade of catching Parrots. Most of those you see in England were taken from the nest, and never knew what it was to be free. The younger the bird, the easier his education will be.

The Indian goes into the forest, and takes some little arrows with blunt points. He only wants to stun the birds, and is anxious not to injure them. He will often try another plan. He will make a fire under the tree, using for fuel a plant, the smoke of which has a strong pungent smell. The poor little birds are stupified with the smoke, and fall to the ground. Then the Indian picks them up, and carries them away.

But, now and then, he has rather an unruly captive. A bird will be sullen, and refuse to eat or to be taught. The Indian has a sure way of punishment. He has only to blow a little tobacco smoke into the eyes of the Parrot, and it is enough. The Parrot has such a dislike to the smell of tobacco, that he will become as docile as possible.

The Indian will often subject his prisoners to very curious treatment. He will try to alter the colour of their plumage, and make it more showy. There is a Parrot, called the Amazonian Parrot, that is one of the best talkers in the whole family. The Indians value him highly, and try to procure him when he is very young, and the feathers are only beginning to grow. They pluck the feathers from the neck and shoulders, and rub the parts with a colouring substance or dye, called anatto. The feathers soon grow again ; but this time, instead of being green, they are a brilliant red or yellow. In fact, the green costume is changed for one much more splendid. But the health of the bird suffers from the treatment he has received. He is feeble and

melancholy, and without any of the sprightliness
of his race. But the Indian can sell him for a
good sum of money, since the transformed birds
are very rare, and much sought after.

There is but one species of Parrot a native
of the United States. It is called the Carolina
Parrot, and feeds upon a plant called the cockle-
bur. The cockle-bur is as abundant as the
Parrots. It grows in the fields, along the banks
of the great American rivers, and ripens after
the harvest has been gathered in. It grows
so thickly, and the burs stick so fast together,
that a man can scarcely force his way through
them. The burs stick to his clothes, and are very
difficult to rub off. And if the man is on horse-
back, they will cling to the horse's tail, and make
it a tangled mass, so that it has to be cut off.
The poor sheep that chances to stray into one of
these fields is in a sorry plight; the wool is
literally torn from its back. And the worst of
the matter is, that the cockle-bur does no good
to outweigh all this mischief. It possesses no
valuable property either as food or as medicine.

But when I use the word food, I am forgetting the Parrots.

The tiresome cockle-burs are a rich harvest on which the Parrots feed with delight.

The Parrot settles on the plant, and plucks the great bur from the stem, using his foot as a hand. He turns the bur about until he gets it in a right position. Then he strikes and tears it with his bill, and soon splits it open. He takes out the contents and eats them, letting the husk drop on the ground. A flock of Parrots will busy themselves in this manner until the field is almost stripped. But, alas! the cockle-bur is by no means destroyed. Up it comes the next spring, as abundant as ever!

Nor can we regard the Parrot as a benefactor. He is nothing of the kind. He is not content with usefully feeding on the cockle-bur. He eats any kind of fruit or of grain that he can get, and is not particular as to the way he procures it.

When the farmer has stored up his stack of corn in the field, you would think he had thrown over it a carpet of brilliant colours. But you are mistaken.   What looks like a carpet is, in reality, a flock of Parrots, dressed in their gaudy plumes.   They stick their claws into the sides of the stack, and hold on while they pick out the straws and get at the grain.   They waste more than they eat, scattering it on the ground all round the stack.

They are very fond of fruit, and they do not wait till it is ripe.   They come in the same brilliant flocks, and fall, like a sheet of colour, on the trees in the orchard, while the pears and apples are young and green.   They pick, and tear, and devour without mercy.   They are quite at their ease on any kind of plant; for they can hook, or swing, or clamber, or put themselves in any posture.   The boughs will be full of them, packed together as closely as possible.

If one of the flock cries out, the rest take fright and fly away, for they are timid just at first.   They will not come again that day; but they will be here again to-morrow; and do not quit the orchard until the trees that looked so fair and flourishing are entirely stripped.

But the farmer is not likely to sit still and see all this mischief go on under his eyes. He takes his gun, and walks into the orchard. The Parrots have overcome their shyness, and are eagerly devouring the fruit, passing from branch to branch, too much occupied to notice him. He begins to shoot, and down drops a Parrot, its bill full of seeds. The rest of the birds seem to lose their senses. They scream, and fly round and round, and are in a great commotion; but they never think of leaving the orchard, although the gun keeps going off every minute. They return to the fruit, even though their companions lie dead on the ground. Indeed, the farmer goes on shooting, until he begins to think he has used as much powder and shot as he can afford.

XIII.

MALACCA PARRAKEET.

HE family of Parrots is a very large one, and includes a great many species. They are chiefly confined to warm countries and the vicinity of the Equator. Here their gaudy plumage seems in harmony with the brilliant and burning sun of the Tropics. But no rule is without an exception; and the range of the Parrots extends farther than was thought. They have been seen flying before a snow-storm along the banks of the Ohio, one of the great American rivers; and Parrots have been met with in Van Diemen's Land.

Naturalists divide this numerous and wide-spread family into groups, and found their divisions on the bill, the tongue, and the feet of the bird.

The bill is differently shaped according to the species. It is longer or shorter, or more or less curved, or its edges are either with or without notches.

The tongue may be thick and fleshy, or it may end in a kind of brush, or it may be merely a hollow and rather horny tube or gland. Sometimes the claws will be short and thick, and the Parrot can run along the ground, instead of always climbing.

There is a group of Parrots which are the most graceful and beautiful of the whole tribe. Their bodies are of an emerald green, and their bills of a deep ruby. Round the neck is a rose-coloured collar. The two middle feathers in the tail reach to a great length, and are of a beautiful blue. The bird itself has a moderately sized bill, the lower mandible short and notched. Its claws are rather weak and slender ; and it goes by the name of the Malacca Parrakeet.

The home of the Parrakeet is in the very heart of the Tropics—a district or country full of beautiful birds and radiant insects. I mean the peninsula of Malacca. There are Trogons, in their rich costume, and with their crimson breasts. There is the curious "Rain-bird," clad in black and maroon, and with white stripes and a bill intensely blue. There are the Toncans, with their immense bills, which look so heavy, but in reality are so light, and carried with such ease. There are brilliant Kingfishers, some of which dart about like a flame of fire. The Kingfishers, I must tell you, have some relations in the islands close by, that are never found near the water. Two of their tail-feathers are immensely long, and spread out at the end like a spoon. The birds are called Kinghunters, to distinguish them from their neighbours that live upon fish. They do not eat fish, but they feed on snails and insects. The Kinghunter spies its prey on the ground, as it sits watching on some branch of a tree. It gives the same sudden dart or swoop that the Kingfisher does, and rarely fails of its object.

The rarest and most beautiful of the Kinghunters is called the Racquet-tailed Kingfisher, and lives in the island of Amboyna. Its red bill and white breast, and deep purple wings, and blue spots, give it a lovely appearance. It bears the palm of beauty even here, where Nature is so profuse of colour, and seems never weary of decorating bird, insect, and flower.

Here, too, in Malacca, are found our friends the Cuckoos, in dresses of green and brown, and rejoicing in perpetual summer. And in the thickest part of the forest a Pheasant, called the Great Argus Pheasant, runs along the ground; but is seldom seen, and rarely caught.

XIV.

THE MANCHINEEL NOT POISON TO THE BIRDS.

THE vast regions of the Tropical forest are as a storehouse in which Nature prepares her ingredients for the good or ill of man —her medicines and her poisons.

Tribes of plants or trees may be called benefactors of mankind, such as the bountiful palm, the banana, and the plantain.

Other families have deadly juices running through their tissues. They are not calculated to bless, but to destroy. Some of these dangerous plants are fair to look upon.

There is a tree which bears a number of bright red apples. The smell of the apples is very pleasant, and a little like the perfume of the lemon. The traveller coming to the tree, weary and thirsty, might be inclined to pluck the fruit, and to think himself fortunate in obtaining such a supply of food. But woe to him if he touches one of those tempting apples! He may not know it, but he has met with the deadliest tree of the Tropics— the manchineel!

It was once thought that to sleep under the shadow of the manchineel was fatal, but this is not the case. Provided the traveller refrains from eating the fruit, he is safe.

Yet even the fruit is less deadly than the milky juice that flows from the trunk when an incision is made. If the juice is swallowed, it destroys life with a rapidity that is frightful. If it does but touch the skin, it causes swellings and irritation; even the vapour arising from it affects the eyes and lips.

In the forest are hosts of plants not less dangerous. There is a kind of spurge, the milk of which, if it get into the eyes, causes blindness. It owes its name to this circumstance.

A sailor was cutting wood in the forest, when his axe struck, by accident, one of these fatal trees. The milky juice that started from the wound touched his eyes, and blinded him.

In the splendour of the forest, amid its glowing flowers and gorgeous recesses, Death seems thus to lurk in every form. Man might turn away in dread, but the bird, on sapphire wing, and with crest of emerald, plunges amid the poisons of Nature, and revels in them. These dangerous shades, where poisonous fruits gleam with a sinister beauty, are haunted by the birds.

The Parrakeet comes to the manchineel for a repast. He devours the red apples with impunity; nay, he has his home amid the branches. Here is his nest, and here he rears his brood in health and vigour.

The poison is not poison to him; it is his natural food.

XV

THE RINGED PARRAKEET.

PERHAPS the most favourite of our pet birds is the one in the Picture. You often see it in a cage. It belongs to a wide-spread group of the Parrakeet family, and is called the Ringed Parrakeet. It is found over a very extensive range of country. You meet with it in Asia, Africa, and Australia. It is very beautiful. Its plumage is green, but the feathers of the head and neck change, as you look at them, into purple. The body is a brilliant red, and it has a ring or collar of ruby.

The Ringed Parrakeet is supposed to be the first of its tribe known to the ancient Greeks.

When Alexander the Great went on his Indian expeditions, he opened the way for many discoveries. The Ringed Parrakeet was soon after brought to Greece. Like the rest of its tribe, it has slender feet, which enable it to run along the ground. It can easily be tamed, and makes a very delightful pet.

In Australia, Parrots and Parrakeets abound in great numbers. They are seen flying in brilliant clouds from tree to tree, or they will rise up before you like a sheet of gems or gold, as their plumage glistens in the sun.

They have as many tricks as the monkeys. A number of them will sit crowded on a branch, fluttering and sidling, and eyeing each other in the drollest manner. And the chattering and the screaming, and the various noises they make, can hardly be described. Some of the houses in Australia have gardens filled with Tropical flowers and fruits. There is the pomegranate and the oleander, and many others which are never seen with us except in a hot-house. And over the verandah the vine grows in full luxuriance. Tro-

pical birds are often kept in the verandah in cages.
Here you see the most lovely Parrakeets. One of
them is called the Painted Lady, and is a native
of Australia.

On each cheek of the bird is a soft crimson spot,
like the delicate bloom on a lady's face. The rest
of the costume is lavender, and the breast is a pale
primrose.

There is a Parrakeet, found in Van Diemen's
Land, which is called the Black-spotted Parrakeet.
Its plumage is green, but the middle tail-feathers
are barred with green and black. The remainder of
the tail-feathers are barred with black and yellow.
Its legs and bill are black. This beautiful and
rare bird is seldom seen. It does not perch on
the trees, like the rest of the Parrots. It lives on
the ground in moist places. When it is alarmed,
it rises up from the grass; but when the danger is
over, it soon drops down again.

I might mention many beautiful birds of this
family.

There is a superb Parrakeet found in Otaheite,
that wears a dress of entire and vivid blue. An-

other, found in India, is of the colour of a peach-
blossom.   And there is a red-winged Parrakeet,
with legs and claws of a rich carnation.

Also, as a contrast to these, there is the Black
Parrot, in a costume of bluish-black; and the
Sapphire Parrot, dressed in green and scarlet, that
lives in the Philippine Islands, and revels in the
juices of the cocoa-nut palm.   It makes a nest
of a peculiar construction, and sets about it very
cunningly.   Its great enemy is the monkey, that
is always on the look-out for plunder.   But the
Parrot is more than a match for him.   The monkey
sees the nest hanging from the tree, and makes his
way to it with great glee, thinking to feast on
eggs ; but when he takes hold of the nest, he finds
the lower part not so closely woven as the upper.
It gives way at once, and down falls the robber
before he has done any mischief.

XVI

BIRDS OF THE SPICE ISLANDS.

YOU have heard many times of the Spice Islands. The name brings with it the idea of fragrance and of beauty. Here grow the clove, the cinnamon, the nutmeg, and all the precious spices of the East.

And here also we come upon a splendid array of birds and insects, such as are rarely met with even in the Tropics.

Here the Parrots abound in vast numbers, and are much sought after. But the native does not lay his snare for them in order to teach them to talk, or to sell them to the European, so much as for another reason. The small Parrakeets that

abound on every hand are a very delicate article
of food. Their flesh tastes of the fragrant berry
or spice on which they feed; and when they are
plump and in their best condition, the hunter
comes to seek for them.

He walks into some lovely grove or wood where
he knows the Parrakeets abound. At first he
looks about, and is not able to see one of them;
for their green plumage is too much the colour of
the leafy bower amid which they sit. He can
hear their various noises, but is unable to distinguish them. It is not, however, the nature of
these restless birds to remain quiet many minutes.
They soon begin to flutter, and to move from
bough to bough. One reason is, that they have
stripped the branch on which they were sitting of
all its berries, and wish to attack another. The
hunter hears a great moving of wings, and rust-
ling, and flying hither and thither. The birds
have come from their safe canopy of leaves, and
can be seen clearly. This is the moment he has
been waiting for. Off goes his gun, and an unlucky Parrakeet is sure to drop to the ground.

The rest of the birds set up a loud screaming; but they do not take their departure until one after another has fallen a victim to the enemy.

Splendid crimson Parrots are found amid these spicy groves. And here, too, is a family of birds of the Parrot tribe, which are called Lories.

The Crimson Lory has plumage of a deep scarlet, that shines with the utmost richness and beauty. The Grand Lory is superb in blue and violet; and the whole of the tribe vie, in their splendid array, with the beautiful birds around them.

Like the Parrots, they can talk and chatter famously when they are taught. The name of the tribe is "Garrulous."

Here, too, in this land of beautiful birds, are the most lovely Pigeons you can imagine; with brilliant patches of colour on their heads, and bearing the name of Fruit-eating Pigeons, because they live on the rich spices of the woods and groves.

There are Cockatoos without number, and Kingfishers of wondrous brilliance and beauty.

And here, also, is a bird, which, though not so beautiful as the rest, is so curious that I cannot pass it over without notice. For we have come to the home and haunt of the wonderful Mound-maker, found here in great abundance.

The traveller in his wanderings often comes on a curious spectacle. He sees a great heap of rubbish, higher than himself, and about twelve feet wide. At first he thinks it is the hut of a native. But as he watches, with some curiosity, forth steps a bird, a little like a Hen, with brown feathers, sometimes banded with red, and with very strong feet and claws.

This is the mound-making bird, a distant relation of our own barn-door fowl. But it has not the same habits. It does not choose to sit on its eggs; but it makes quite another arrangement.

It lives near the sea-shore, in bushy places where there is a kind of jungle, and where it can pick up sticks and sea-weed, and all kinds of rubbish from the beach. Of these materials the birds make their great mound, and bury their eggs in it. There is a warmth arising from the decaying matter of which the mound is made, and this is sufficient to hatch the eggs. When the little ones come out of their shell, they work their way out of their prison, and run off to the forest. The natives have a great fancy for the eggs of the mound-making bird, and are always on the watch to rob the nest. They know by certain signs whether the mound is full or empty. If it is full, they break in and steal its contents.

THE LORIES.

———◆———

HERE is a family of Parrots found in Australia that differ from the rest of the tribe.

They are called Lorikeets, and you see one of them in the Picture. They are very handsome, as you perceive, and wear a costume of red and green, and blue and yellow. And they have the hooked bill of the Parrot, and cling to the branches, and climb and swing, as he does.

But the Lorikeet does not lead exactly the same life as the Parrot. He does not live on the same food. Not fruit, but honey tempts him.

Honey is the chief means of his subsistence, and he is always in search of it.

His tongue is not like the tongue of the Parrot, for it is used in a different manner. He does not want a great fleshy organ to assist in holding and cracking nuts. He does not eat nuts. He wants a light, brush-like tongue, covered with bristles to sweep off the honey; and therefore Nature has given him one. Not any of the Parrot tribe are possessed of the tongue of the Lorikeet, for it would be useless to them.

The Lorikeet leads a very happy life among the honied sweets that surround him. Many delicious blossoms abound on every hand. Here are orange-groves in their full beauty, and the scarlet flowers of the pomegranate display their stores. But the Lorikeet delights in those flowers which grow on the tallest trees; and there are numbers of these to be found.

There is the mighty gum-tree, the giant of the country, that grows to an immense height. And there is the peppermint-tree, which, at the proper season, is a mass of blossom. Then myriads of birds flock round it to rifle its sweets, and to sport around them, showering down bunches of flowers as if in play. The Lorikeet feeds so greedily, and is so intent on satisfying his hunger, that an enemy may approach very near without being perceived. Nay, the fatal gun may be pointed at him, and yet he will not stir. After he has been shot, he will yet cling to the branch; for his claws have grasped so tightly that they will not all at once relax their hold.

When he drops to the ground, or is picked from the bough, his crop is full of honey. The native is as fond of sweets as the bird is, and he puts the head of the poor Lorikeet in his mouth, and sucks the honey out through the beak.

I should tell you that the name Lory has been given to this tribe of Parrots, because they have the habit of saying the word "Lory" over and over again.

XVIII.

THE PRINCE OF THE PARROTS, AND THE LOVE-BIRDS.

HAVE yet more to say about the Parrots. There is a bird of the tribe that may be considered as the prince or emperor of the whole race. I mean the Macaw. He is of the family of the Parrots, but he is distinguished by having no feathers on the sides of his face. And he has a long tail, almost like a Peacock's.

He leads very much the same life, among the boughs and branches of the Tropical forest, that the Parrots do. But though the plumage of the Parrot shines and glistens, that of the Macaw is much more splendid. He is larger than the Parrot, and the flaming scarlet of his body is more striking. His wings are red, yellow, blue, and green,—all blended in the most beautiful manner, and as vivid as possible. His long, splendid tail-feathers are scarlet and blue.

The traveller, when he comes in sight of this magnificent bird, feels compelled to stop and admire. And the Macaw would be courted and caressed, like the Parrot, and perhaps have his place in the houses of the great and the noble, but for his voice.

His voice is a loud harsh scream, that almost deafens you, and forces you to keep him at a distance. The Macaw loves to feed upon the fruit of the palm-trees. A flock of these splendid birds will cover the fruit-bearing boughs like a glittering carpet. The native takes his blow-pipe or · his poisoned arrow, and kills as many of them as he likes. But their screams and their noise are scarcely to be borne, and are enough to drive the enemy away.

Their habits are those of the Parrots. They fly

in flocks, and have their nests in the hollows of the trees.

When a flock of some thousand Macaws are flying in the rays of the setting sun, the sight can hardly be described. It is like a mantle of flaming red.

The natives take the feathers of the Macaw to wear as an ornament, and they use the flesh as food.

As this gorgeous Parrot is the head of his tribe, so the Love-Bird is the smallest of the family.

He, too, is a kind of Parrot, and the most affectionate of any. The love of the Parrot for his companions is the best feature in his character. The Love-Bird possesses this trait in such a degree that he has earned the name of Love-Bird, from his loving and caressing ways. He tenderly cherishes his companion during life; and if bereaved, by death, nothing can exceed his grief. He will pine away, and die.

Nay, if compelled to be alone, he will droop and decline. He cannot exist without the society of his fellows.

His plumage gives him a place among the "beautiful birds." It is green, but touched and tinted with a deep rich blue. His tail-feathers are scarlet, with a band of black, and the tip of the feathers are green. The appearance and manners of the Love-Birds are very interesting. They sit close together on a bough, as you see them do in the Picture, nestling and caressing each other with the utmost affection.

Their home is in the southern part of Africa; but they are much sought after as pets, and are brought to England as the most elegant ornament for a lady's boudoir.

XIX.

THE COCKATOO.

HE Parrot has a number of relations, distinguished by the elegant head-dress they wear. This is a crest or tuft of beautiful feathers, which can be lifted up or allowed to fall down at pleasure.

These elegant birds are called Cockatoos, and you see one of them in the Picture. It has its crest set up, and its feathers are white, with a tinge of red.

The Cockatoos love the damp recesses of the forest, and, like other beautiful birds, are children of the Tropics. But, like their relations the Parrots, they often do a great deal of mischief. They are not satisfied with the forest fruits, but come flying abroad to see what else they can obtain. The rice-plantations suffer much from their visits. They come in flocks of eight hundred or more at a time, and settle on the field. They not only devour the rice, but spoil as much as they eat, breaking and tearing everything around them.

The owner of the plantation may well look upon them as pests, and do all he can to destroy them. In Australia, the natives often have a day's sport in hunting the Cockatoos.

The birds fly in flocks along the banks of the river, and are very shy and easily alarmed. But the native is skilful and patient, and knows what to do. First of all, he watches near some stream until he sees a flock of Cockatoos in the air. Great trees surround the stream, and here the birds settle to take their evening's nap.

This matter of going to roost is not to be done all at once. There is a vast amount of screaming and fluttering, and flying from tree to tree, before they settle. The native creeps cautiously along, making not a sound. He even puts aside his clothing, lest it should hinder or embarrass him.

He steals from tree to tree, and bush to bush, in the same noiseless manner; but, with all his care, he cannot escape the watchful eye of the sentinel birds. The flock takes alarm, and flies to the tree nearest the water, getting close together, and as if aware that some danger is near.

At length the native comes close to the water's edge, and the Cockatoos see him plainly. They utter loud cries, and spring into the air as if to escape. Now is the time for the native to draw his kiley, or spear, from his belt. He flings it with violence, and it flies from his hand as if about to touch the surface of the water. But it does not do so. It spins upwards in a wonderful manner, and darts through the air, making all kinds of turns and twists, in each of which it is sure to strike a Cockatoo.

The weapon, when flung in this manner, seems for the moment to be alive; and the more the frightened birds try to escape, the more they seem to come in its way. Many of them fall with loud screams to the ground.

But the native is not satisfied. He knows the

habits of the Cockatoo, and that it is most affectionate to its companions. He picks up a wounded bird, and fastens it to a tree. He is certain what will happen. When the birds that have flown off hear the piteous cries of their friend, they come back to see what is the matter.

Then again flies the terrible kiley, and one at least of the birds pays for its friendship with its life. I must tell you that the Cockatoos in Australia make their nests in the decayed boughs of trees. The mother-bird lays two eggs, of pure white. Under the tree there is generally to be seen a heap of bark, split up into shreds. The old birds have gathered twigs from the neighbouring trees for their young, stripped off the bark, and let the shreds fall on the ground.

This is rather an unlucky habit. The native is fond of young Cockatoos, and thinks them a delicate dish. He comes prowling about to find the nest, and the little heap of bark is sure to point out the spot.

XX.

THE PINK COCKATOO AND THE GREAT BLACK COCKATOO.

———◆———

THE Cockatoo is usually robed in white, with a rosy tint. But there is an exception to every rule. The bird in the Picture has, as you see, a coloured crest of red and yellow. He is called the Tricolorcrested Cockatoo, and also the Pink Cockatoo. When his crest is set up it is very beautiful, and looks like rays of crimson, white, and gold.

But he has a relation that is far more wonderful and more rare than he is. I mean the Great Black Cockatoo. He is the exception I spoke of.

Amid the white-robed, rosy-tinted family, he alone is dressed in sable plumage.

He is found in Australia, the land of Cockatoos, and also in the Aru Islands, the home, as you know, of the Birds of Paradise.

His body is weak and small, and his legs are feeble. But his wings are large, and he has a monstrous head, with a splendid crest of black feathers. His cheeks are a livid red, and he has a strong sharp bill, that is capable of any amount of work.

He does not make a screaming noise, like the rest of his tribe, but he has a low, plaintive whistle. His tongue is a deep red colour, and is like a tube with a curious horny plate at the end of it. He can stretch or thrust out his tongue to some distance, and is altogether the most curious specimen of his race.

In Australia, the Black Cockatoos will settle now and then on one of the great gum-trees I have spoken about. There they sidle up and down the branches, after the true Parrot fashion, and move their handsome top-knots up and down, as if bowing to each other. But they are not very common; indeed, the Black Cockatoo is considered a rare bird, like a neighbour of his, also found in Australia—the Black Swan.

In the forests of the Aru Islands, the Black Cockatoo is more frequently seen alone, or with one or two companions. His flight is slow and noiseless, and he dies from a very slight wound. He feeds upon the forest nuts, and the fruits and seeds that abound on every hand. But he has one favourite article of food, — the seeds of the kanary-nut. These nuts grow on a lofty tree, and have a smooth shell, as hard as iron.

The Cockatoo takes the nut, which is of a three-cornered shape, in his bill, and holds it fast by means of his tongue, while he saws a slit with the lower part of his bill. Then he takes the nut with his foot and bites off part of a leaf. The leaf is to keep the very smooth shell from slipping about, while he inserts into it the sharp point of his bill, and picks out the kernel bit by bit with his tongue.

No other bird could master such a shell; but the strength and cunning of the Black Cockatoo open the storehouse of food that is fast locked from the rest of the birds.

XXI

THE TROGON.

———◆———

N the sunny regions of the Tropics, Nature seems to preserve her freshness and beauty without interruption. There are no chilling winds or nipping frosts to scatter the foliage of the forest. As one leaf withers, another takes its place, so that the green canopy is always full and compact. There is neither autumn nor winter, but perpetual summer reigns.

In some parts of South America, unbroken forest extends for an immense distance. Brooks and streams run hither and thither in the deep recesses, and are bridged over by Nature with the

trunks of trees that have fallen across by accident.
The ground is covered with a dense carpet of moss
and of decaying leaves, that have lain there undisturbed for centuries. The forest fruits lie scattered in profusion. Here and there you would
see what appears to be a wooden cup or vessel.
At the top of the cup is a hole, into which a round
lid fits with exactness. The cup grew on one of
the loftiest trees of the forest. It contained some
nuts, that in process of time became too heavy
to remain suspended. Then the lid of the cup
loosened itself, and the cup, large and heavy as it
was, fell to the ground with a crash. The nuts
were scattered far and wide, and many of them
served as food for the wild beasts of the forest.
The great empty cup goes by the name of the
Monkey's Drinking-Cup, and is quite a curiosity.

There is another tree which bears a cup, without
a lid. In this instance the nuts fall to the ground
entire, and are not scattered. Many of them are
brought to England, and you have often seen
them. They are called Brazil-nuts. The natives
pick them up, and bring them to the market for

sale. The trees I have just mentioned are very lofty; but here and there in these deep forests you meet with giants. A mighty trunk will tower up, of a size and thickness that can scarcely be believed. This giant trunk takes up a vast space of ground. It will be sixty feet in circumference, and a hundred feet in height.

Like a vast dome, its mighty branches stretch themselves abroad,—the dome of some cathedral built by the hand of Nature.

Silence reigns at times in the forest depths, a silence that becomes oppressive. There is no note of bird or of insect, and the feeling is of utter solitude and isolation. But the forest sounds are only suspended; they have not ceased. Presently a wild yell or scream will startle the forest echoes. A smaller animal has fallen a prey to a larger one, and is uttering its death-cry; or there will be a crash that resounds far and wide with a deafening noise. Some mighty bough, long since decayed, or some tree, has fallen prone on the earth. At intervals, the howling monkeys will burst out with a chorus of unearthly and discordant noises

that cannot be described. And many sounds besides come up from the forest depths that cannot
very well be explained, and the Indian tells you
they are made by the wild man of the woods—a
creature like a monkey, and that lives in the trees.

He will even be afraid to venture far, lest he
should meet with this imaginary being.

I have brought you to this part of the world to
show you a beautiful bird called the Trogon.
Here he is in the Picture, with his splendid green
plumage and crimson breast.

His foot is, as you see, like that of the Parrot,
and he clasps the branch on which he is sitting, as
the Parrot does. His bill is stout and strong, and
has saw-like edges. His beautiful plume of loose
waving feathers—white, and black, and green—
delights the eye.

But his wings, though so beautiful, are feeble.
He does not keep on the wing, nor has he the
agility of the Parrot. He sits quietly on some
low branch in the gloomy shades of the forest,
eyeing the tempting fruit around him. The effort
to obtain it is more than he likes; but presently,

as if impelled by hunger, he makes a dart, seizes it, and conveys it to the branch, where he again settles himself while he is eating it.

After a long pause he repeats the effort, and so by degrees satisfies his hunger.

He is very solitary and rather mournful in his habits. Now and then he utters a plaintive cry; but his greatest pleasure seems to be in dozing lazily on his branch. He dozes sometimes a little too long, for a passer-by, if there be one in so remote a spot, will knock him off his perch and carry him away captive.

You must not think that the Trogon lives only on fruit. He has no objection to insects, and watches them, as they flit about, in the same grave and solemn manner.

By-and-by he bestirs himself, and darts after them with surprising agility. But he will be sure very soon to return to his perch. He cannot fly far; his flowing plumes impede his progress. He will, however, migrate from one part of the country to the other. He arrives at the end of his journey when some particular fruit is ripe of which he is fond.　He remains till the fruit is over, and then goes back again.

The mother Trogon makes her nest in some decayed tree, as the Parrot does.　The eggs lie on a bed of sawdust, made by one of the forest ants. Indeed, the Trogon often takes possession of the ant's nest, and enlarges it and adapts it for her own purpose.

A Trogon has been seen clinging to the bark of a tree, after the fashion of the Woodpecker, digging all the time with his bill, while his partner sat by, watching him as quietly as possible.

XXII.

THE KING'S BIRDS.

————

THE Trogon has some relations in India that have smooth bills, with no saw-like notches upon them. But near the tip of the upper part of the beak is a kind of hook.

All round the eye there is a bare space without feathers, but of a rich colour; and the plumage of the tail is not barred with black and white, like the bird you see in the Picture.

The bird in the Picture lives in Mexico, and is arrayed in a most gorgeous manner. Among the Humming-Birds and brilliant creatures in that Tropical land, he shines and glistens with surpassing beauty.

The lustre of his green plumes can hardly be described, and under his body is a vivid sheet of scarlet. Round his neck is a white ring, and his tail-feathers are barred with black and white and green.

Like the rest of his tribe, he is not often seen. He loves to hide in some deep, cool recess, where he watches patiently for his prey. His food consists both of fruit and of insects, which he catches with his bill.

He has a relation that prefers the fruits to the insects. This splendid bird is the most magnificent of the whole family, and well deserves his name—the Resplendent Trogon.

There he is in the Picture, in his full beauty, sitting on the branch, which he clasps with his feet. His costume is a golden-green, more beautiful than you can imagine, and the scarlet of his breast is dazzling. Do you notice the length of his tail-feathers, and the curve they make, and the white and black bars which appear under the long sweeping plumes?

Age after age these superb creatures of the

forest have lived in successive generations in the
Tropical and flowery land of Mexico. Long time
ago Mexico was a kingdom ruled by its own
monarch, and rich in gold and silver and precious
stones. In those days the palace of the sovereign
might almost be called a palace of gold; and the
pomp and splendour of the court baffled description. But perhaps the fairest and loveliest among
the palace possessions was the collection of beautiful birds kept there in all their living splendour.

The king had two great houses fitted up for
this purpose, and the utmost pains and care were
taken to supply the captives with food and every
necessary. A staff of attendants was employed to
watch over them; and you will smile when I tell
you that a number of doctors were always at hand
to give advice or medicine in case the birds were
sick.

A brilliant assembly indeed were the birds.
Here were Trogons, Humming-Birds, Parrots,
Pigeons, and Sun-Birds. And here, distinct from
these, were all the birds of prey and the water-
fowl, and every feathered creature that could be

procured ; so that the Spaniards, we are told, were astonished and full of admiration at the sight. But not only the sight of the birds was marvellous ; the use made of their feathers was equally curious and wonderful.

The ancient Mexicans thought no costume so lovely as that worn by the birds, and they took the gorgeous feathers and lovely plumes and wove them into mantles and stuffs, and all kinds of dresses, mixing the feathers with gold and silver.

The monarch himself chose the resplendent plumes of the Trogon for a head-dress. So highly were they esteemed in those days, that no one, except he was of the blood-royal, was permitted to wear them.

Persons were appointed on purpose to look after the feathers of the King's Birds. And it was their office to pluck them, and also to weave them into the rich mantles and shining costumes worn by the grandees of the nation.

XXIII.

THE BELL-BIRD.

———

HE great Tropical forest, with its wonderful array of trees, and plants, and living creatures, has been the favourite spot where we have come to look for the beautiful birds. But at times the traveller may look for them in vain. They seem to have taken their departure, and silence reigns in bush and tree. This does not last for long. All at once the bird life begins again with its usual activity. Tree and bush swarm with birds of the most brilliant costume. The Tanagers perch and climb gaily as ever. The solemn Trogon appears in his resplendent plumes seated on some branch in silent ma-

(393) 8

jesty. The Humming-Birds flash, and dart, and sparkle, with all the brilliance and beauty of the Tropics. The deserted spot will be a scene of loveliness and of activity. Among the bevy of beautiful birds now swarming around us, there are some adorned with the utmost splendour, and which we have not yet noticed. They cannot live except under the full heat of the Tropics. The moist, hot parts of the forest are their home; and here they are seen shining in tints and hues that delight the eye of the traveller. One is dressed in the most vivid scarlet, another in blue and violet, a third wears a costume of varied colours harmoniously blended. They do not associate in flocks, but you catch sight of each one, apart from his companions, in the foliage of some shadowy tree, or by some creek or stream; for they delight in the water. Their food is the never-failing fruit of the forest, and their size is that of a small Pigeon. They are called Cotingas.

The Cotinga has no song. Among the forest's notes and sounds he is mute; the gift of music has not been bestowed upon him. But in the early morning, or in the hush of noontide, the traveller may chance to hear a deep full toll, like the sound of a bell. He listens, and again he hears it, loud, clear, and distinct. Then he knows that some three miles distant, on the top of a lofty tree, the wonderful Bell-Bird is sitting. He is related to the brilliant Cotingas, but very unlike them. His plumage is snow-white, and he is about the size of a Jay. On his forehead, and growing from it, is a spiral tube about three inches long. When the bird is alarmed, the tube fills with air, and stands up like a horn. At other times it hangs down.

The Bell-Bird is called by another name. The Spaniards speak of him as the Campanero. His place of abode is South America, and his habits and the mode of building his nest are not known.

The brilliant family of Cotingas are not noticed in any way by their curious relation. He is never seen with them, and might belong to a distinct tribe.

XXIV

THE PARADISE FLY-CATCHER.

HERE is a bird which comes and goes every summer, and is a bird of passage, like the Swallow and the Cuckoo.

It is not very common, but is more often seen in the northern counties of England than in any other part of our island. When August comes, and while the winter is yet a great way off, it takes its departure. The colours it wears are white, and brown, and gray. It has not the radiant hues of the Tropics, and yet it belongs to a Tropical family. We call it the Fly-catcher.

Its relations are scattered far and wide. One of them is found as far north as Siberia and

Kamtschatka, and is called the Dun Fly-catcher. But, as a rule, the Fly-catchers inhabit the warmer parts of the globe; and, like the beautiful birds we have been describing, they revel under the burning sun of the Tropics.

They are called Tyrants; and the group they belong to is termed *Tyranninae*. This is because of their fierce and combative temper, which, as we shall see presently, causes them to tyrannize over birds much larger than themselves.

The bird in the Picture goes by the name of the Paradise Fly-catcher. He wears a green crest, while his bill is of a deep blue. The feathers of his head are green, and his body is white and gray. He has a wedge-shaped tail, and the two middle feathers are, as you see, of a great length. He lives in very hot countries, in India and in Africa.

In India the traveller will often come on a dense thicket of bamboo; for the bamboo, though really a grass, will grow to the size of a magnificent tree. It shoots up in clumps or clusters, rising to the height of eighty or a hundred feet. The stem is hollow, and at intervals forms the same knots or joints that are found in the grasses. From each joint springs a set of branches, which strike out at right-angles to the stem ; and these divide into others, and so on, until the last branch ends in a leaf. In the thicket I am describing all these different branches form a compact mass, crossing and recrossing each other, like a gigantic piece of net-work. At the top of the stem, there droop gracefully over, the lovely plumes of the bamboo, which are of the brightest green, and curl like feathers.

A forest of bamboo is one of the most wonderful sights in nature.

The Indian uses the bamboo for every purpose. He makes his house, his bows and arrows, his furniture, all his possessions, in fact, of bamboo. And the glorious thicket of bamboo is like a vast awning for the beautiful birds of the Tropics. Under its deep cool shadow they can live and rejoice.

The Paradise Fly-catchers make their home here, as in a bower.

They feed on the insects that abound on every

hand. The bird perches on some lofty branch, and watches patiently till its prey shall appear in sight. Presently some insect, perhaps a gorgeous butterfly, or one of the numerous insects of the forest, comes fluttering by. Then the Fly-catcher makes a sudden swoop, and you hear, a moment after, a sharp snap with its beak. You know then that the poor insect is seized and devoured, and the Tyrant is on the watch for another. Sometimes it will hunt on the branch for the beetles or ants that may be crawling about, and pick them off with its bill.

It is not always content with its leafy home of bamboo. It will visit the gardens, and shrubberies, and plantations, in search of prey; and having made a circuit, come back again. There are numbers of Fly-catchers, of different names, and wearing different costumes.

In the Tropical parts of America they swarm in great numbers, as the Sparrows do with us. The trees are full of them, each bird intent on its own business of darting after insects, and taking little notice of its companions. At one season the great mounds of earth made by the ants send out colonies of winged ants. Then the Fly-catchers come prepared for a banquet, and assemble in thousands.

They do not always content themselves with insects; the larger species of birds will even feed on fish. A gentleman was once sitting at his window, and he heard a splash in a lake close by. Looking out, he spied a Fly-catcher perched on a dead branch which overhung the water. A moment after, he saw the bird give a plunge, in the same manner as the Kingfisher does. Then it rose again to its branch, and sat, as if drying its feathers. The gentleman watched intently, and he saw the bird dive again into the water, and bring up a tiny fish, just after the manner of the Kingfisher. The dart was made with the rapidity of lightning, and then the bird sat on the branch, as if to allow its feathers to dry.

The Fly-catcher has even been suspected of devouring small animals, for a lizard was once found in its stomach.

XXV

THE KING-BIRD.

ONE of the Fly-catchers goes by the name of the King-Bird. This title has been given to him because of his behaviour all the time his mate is sitting on her eggs.

At this season, his life is one series of fierce battles and quarrels. He quarrels with every bird that ventures near to his nest, and darting out, gives instant battle.

It matters not to what species the bird belongs. Hawks, Crows, even the Eagle himself is certain to be attacked. And such is the valour of the King-Bird, that he is sure to be the victor.

The moment he catches sight of his enemy,

out he sallies, and rises high in the air. Then he drops suddenly down on the Eagle's back.

The royal bird, surprised to find himself thus attacked, makes efforts to get rid of the burden. He wheels about, and tries by turns and swoops to shake off his rider. But the Fly-catcher sits firm, and rises only to descend again with greater violence. By his shrill cries and tormenting attacks he drives the Eagle far away from the nest.

The birds cannot be expected to feel any great liking for such a resolute little tyrant. The King-Bird is not at all popular among his feathered companions; and now and then the tables are turned.

There is a pretty kind of Swallow, called the Purple Martin, that is a match for him. The wings of the Martin can bear him farther, and are stronger and swifter, than those of the Fly-catcher. He can elude all his attacks, and curve, and sweep, or dart, keeping safe out of his way, and yet provoking him into a rage.

A pair of Martins once built in the same tree

on which a pair of King-Birds were rearing their young. As might be supposed, the battles between the two families were endless. No sooner had the mother Fly-catcher begun to sit upon her eggs than the Martin attacked her mate with great violence. The King-Bird fought with his usual bravery, and the conflict lasted for several days. At last, the poor King-Bird was struck to the ground so many times, and with such force, that he died. Then it was an easy matter to drive away his forlorn partner, and the Martins had the tree to themselves.

The Great Red-headed Woodpecker does not tamely submit to the violence of the King-Bird. On the contrary, he amuses himself by teasing him, and playing a kind of bo-peep round the trunk of a tree near to the place where the nest is situated, and where the Woodpecker is searching for insects.

Out darts the furious King-Bird ; but the Woodpecker is far too nimble. He disappears behind the trunk in. a minute. But when the baffled King-Bird has returned to his nest, back

comes the Woodpecker; and his great red head
plays bo-peep again, as if it were the greatest
fun possible.

All the fury of the King-Bird is put on while
the young ones are in the nest, and in order to
protect them from danger. When the young
birds are fledged, and there is no more occasion
to fight, he becomes mild and gentle, and declines
any further combats.

He is exceedingly fond of honey, and does a
great deal of mischief among the bee-hives. He
goes into some garden where there is a row of
hives. Then he plants himself on the fence, or
on the branch of a tree. The poor bees are as
busy as usual, collecting their golden stores; and
they come humming by, never suspecting any
danger. But out darts the King-Bird, and seizes
one of them in his bill. He does so every instant, and puts numbers of bees to death. Then
he even seizes on their golden stores of honey.

The Fly-catchers appear in the United States
of America early in the spring, intending to pass
the summer there. They have had a long jour-

ney from the more Tropical regions, and seem at first rather fatigued, and utter no sound or note. But they soon recover themselves, and make a sharp, tremulous cry, which is heard in the fields and woods.

They do not like the deep shades of the forest, but choose orchards, or sweet-smelling clover-fields, or even gardens, close by the dwellings of man, and where insects abound.

When they have chosen their partners, they set about building the nest.

They make choice of a branch that shoots out in a convenient manner from the tree. Then they pick up a few twigs to fix upon it, and make a beginning. Next, they fly about seeking for bits of hemp, or wool, or cotton, or whatever they can find ; and they are not particular where they get it from.

They place it in thick layers or rows, and make a good strong fabric. They line the nest with hair or fibrous roots ; and when it is finished, the mother-bird lays her eggs.

Then her partner begins to keep watch, and to

fight all those furious battles we have been describing.

If you would like to have some idea of his
appearance, and the costume he wears, I can tell
you. His costume is soft and glossy, and the
upper part is of a bluish-gray. His tail is black,
tipped with white. There is a bright flame-
coloured patch on his head, that looks very gay;
and his breast is white.

He has a curious manner of flying. As he
moves slowly over the field, he makes a vibration
with his wings in the same manner as the Hawk
does.

Sometimes he hovers like the Hawk, or he dives
down to the rich blossoms of the clover, as if to
sip their sweetness. Then he ascends, snapping
his bill, and making graceful curves in the air,
as he darts after various insects.

Sometimes he takes his stand on a tall weed,
near which cattle are grazing. Then he waits
patiently, his eye following the movements of
the troublesome flies that come to attack the herd.

All at once he sees a fly that looks very tempting. He makes a dart, and secures it. Then he returns to the same spot to watch for more.

In the beginning of the autumn, while the weather is yet warm, the Fly-catchers form themselves into groups, and fly silently and in the night to some spot where the winter cannot come.

The young birds, who are now in full plumage, join the party. But they meet with enemies on their track. The flesh of the bird is esteemed by many persons as a delicacy; and they are shot down as they fly.

XXVI

THE STRANGE EGG IN THE NEST.

———◆———

E have not quite done with the Fly-catchers. They are too numerous a family to be dismissed without a little farther notice.

There is the Great Crested Fly-catcher, that lives in the woods, and has no powers of song, but makes a harsh squeak. Now and then, he visits the orchards, and comes in search of the bees in the garden. But he is not fond of fighting, nor has he the courage of his relation the King-Bird.

He feeds as much on berries, as on insects; and he makes his nest in the hollow of a tree, where a Woodpecker has once lived. The materials for the nest are very scanty. But, mixed with them, is always a piece of snake-skin, cast off by the reptile when he changes his coat, and which is readily met with in the forest. The nest has never been seen without it; and it forms a soft, silky bed for the young to lie upon. It has even been thought that the sight of the snake-skin coiled round the nest may have the effect of driving away intruders.

The most welcome of all the Fly-catchers is a bird called the Peewit.

When the Peewit is heard to utter his note, the gardener may begin to plant his peas and beans, and to sow his onions and radishes. The cold weather is sure to be over then.

The Peewit loves to haunt streams and rivers, and to build his nest under the arch of a bridge or in a cave. The nest is made of mud mixed with wax, and is lined with hair and with flax. He will sit on some twig close by, while the young are being hatched, and utter his peculiar cry of " Pee-wit, pee-wit."

His note has no music in it, and yet it always gladdens the ear.   Like the note of the Cuckoo in England, it is associated with the bright days of spring, and the opening flowers.

In the middle of the summer his song partly ceases.   In the autumn he gives a few notes by way of farewell, and then retreats before the winter.

The Peewit wears a loose crest on his head, and his wings and tail are of a dusky hue.   The lower part of his body is of a pale yellow, and his legs and bill are black.

He has a neighbour, called the Wood Peewit, that lives in the gloomy shades of the woods, and chooses some spot where the trees are decaying, and great dead branches shoot across the path.

He is a very clever Fly-catcher.   He sits on the high dead bough of some tree, uttering a plaintive note.   Now and then he gives a dart or sweep after some insect that happens to come near.

Though he loves the forest, he will often venture to the city, and carry on his fly-catching business close to the houses and gardens.

The smallest of the Fly-catchers is not much bigger than the Humming-Bird; and it is one of the nurses chosen by a bird called the Cow-Bunting to bring up her offspring.

The Cow-Bunting has very much the habits of the Cuckoo. For some reason or other, which no one can yet understand, she does not make a nest, or hatch her eggs. But she fixes on a few of her neighbours', and goes from nest to nest, dropping an egg in each. The movements of the Cow-Bunting have been closely watched by the naturalist. He has seen her flit from bush to bush, and copse to copse, seeking the nests suitable for her purpose.

You would not suppose the nest of the little Fly-catcher would be strong enough to hold the egg. The materials are of the most fragile kind —a few old leaf-stalks, a withered blossom or two, and the stem of a fern, covered over with dry lichen, and lined with horse-hair. This is all.

The nest itself is placed on the branch of a

tree, and seems scarcely large enough to contain its owner.   But the Cow-Bunting approaches, drops her egg into the frail habitation, and departs.

The tiny Fly-catchers, returning from their hunt after insects—a hunt carried on from the tops of the tallest trees—find the egg in the nest. They are for a little time rather excited; but they allow the egg to remain.   Nay, the little Fly-catcher hatches and brings up the young Cow-Bunting.

In the meantime, her own eggs have disappeared.   This is always the case when the strange egg has been dropped into the nest.   The eggs of the foster-parents vanish before it, and no one has yet found out what becomes of them.

XXVII

SUN-BIRDS.

———————

THE Sun-Birds have been called by old writers the Humming-Birds of Africa.

Africa is the home of a vast variety of these beautiful birds. They are distinguished from each other by many marks and signs, pointing out the different species. But in all instances the plumage is brilliant, and the under surface of the body is adorned with bands or stripes of colour.

The name of the family is *Nectarinidæ*, and has been given them from their habit of sipping the nectar of flowers; indeed, they were once supposed to live entirely on honey. But this is not the case, since insects form part of their diet.

The other title of "Sun-Bird" has been given to this radiant little creature because of the wonderful effect of the sunlight on its feathers.

They change colour every moment, and flash and sparkle in a manner not to be described. This effect is produced by the bird itself. It has the power of changing the position of its feathers by a movement of its muscles, and so throwing them into a different light, or exhibiting a portion of the surface hitherto concealed.

The Sun-Bird does not feed on the wing, or hover over the flower, as the Humming-Bird does. It settles on the petals, and puts in its long bill; or it clambers about and suspends itself in the attitude most favourable for getting access to the flower. The bill has some tiny notches or teeth, so small that they cannot be seen except through a microscope. This shows that the prey has to be seized and held, and that the bird does not feed entirely on honey. It is true that the long beak is plunged into the chalice of the flower, as into a goblet of honey; but the bird pecks out the insects found therein, and banquets on them as well as on the juices of the flower. Sometimes, indeed, the Sun-Bird is seen clambering about the leaves and branches of the dwarf trees and the brushwood. There no honey can be found, and the sole object of the search is for insects.

As the bird passes from flower to flower, it utters a shrill, impatient cry. But when it is warbling to its mate, its note will be sweet and pleasant. But it is so low, that unless you stood under the tree where the bird was perching, you could not hear its song.

The Sun-Bird makes her nest of the down of plants mixed with a few dead leaves, and the outside wall is all of moss. It looks, when it is finished, like a little ball, rather pointed at the bottom; and the bird makes a cover for it, like a hood, that hides the hole where she enters, and prevents it being seen.

Sometimes she will build her nest in the hollow of a tree, or else suspend it to a twig, and let it hang in the air, as the Tailor-Bird does.

And—what you will think very strange—she
has even been known to fix it to a spider's web !
The spiders that live in hot countries are very
large and strong, and their webs are more like
gauze than cobwebs. So the tiny nest of the
Sun-Bird, as light as a feather, may very well be
fixed to one of them without breaking the threads.

Nothing can be more gaudy than these brilliant
little creatures, that sport about with the gaily-
dressed birds of the Tropics. And, like most
other birds, they put on their best attire at that
season of the year when they choose their partners,
and begin to think of building their nests. Then
their brightest tints are worn, and they are orna-
mented with tufts and crests that afterwards dis-
appear. Indeed, on this occasion they are said
to wear " their wedding-dress."

THE COLLARED SUN-BIRD.

THE bird in the Picture is one of the most lovely specimens of its race.

It is called the Collared Sun-Bird, and lives near the Cape of Good Hope. Very little is known of its habits; but it is supposed to build in the hollows of trees, or, where the country is more open, in some bush or shrub.

It is a creature of exquisite beauty. The golden - green of its plumage changes every moment you behold it. Under the green of the breast is a band of steel-blue, and then a band of glowing crimson. On either side of the crimson band or stripe is a tuft of bright yellow feathers.

The wings are glossed with green, and the upper
feathers of the tail are violet.   You can scarcely
imagine the effect produced by a number of these
gorgeous birds, as they sit perched on the petals
of some brilliant spike of flowers, or as they
glitter and sparkle in the sun.   There is a relation
of the Collared Sun-Bird that is, if possible, more
magnificent.   It is called the Double-collared
Sun-Bird, and is much larger than the bird we
have been describing.   It has the same arrangement of colours, but the blue band is of a deeper
tint, and the crimson stripe is broader.   It lives
in Africa, and chooses the forests that clothe the
eastern side of the continent.   Now and then, it
descends into the plains, but it makes its nest in
the hollow of some forest tree; and the mother-
bird lays four or five eggs.

There is still another Collared Sun-Bird, a
dried specimen of which has been brought to
England.   It is so much like the bird in the
Picture, that for a long time the two were thought
to be the same.

The only difference between them is, that in

the bird of which I am speaking the wings and tail are smaller, and the beautiful collar of blue is wanting. The upper feathers of the tail are of the same brilliant green as the head and back, instead of being violet. This beautiful bird is found in Africa, near the river Niger.

Nothing can exceed the grandeur of the African trees. Some of them are of a gigantic size, and have existed for ages.

One of these trees, vast as it is, belongs to the same family as the mallow and the hollyhock, and has the same mild juices.

The African gathers the leaves, and when he has dried and pounded them, mixes the powder with his food. He also makes a strong cordage of the fibres of the bark.

The baobab, or monkey-bread tree, as it is called, will often be stripped of its bark to a considerable distance up the stem. But this seems not to harm the tree, and merely causes it to throw out a new bark.

As the baobab begins to decay, the hollow space in the trunk fills with water, that is protected from the sun, and keeps cool and fresh for a long time.

The natives come to this supply as to a fountain. They sometimes bring buckets made of leather, and, climbing the tree, let down a bucket and draw as much as they require.

This is not the only use made of the baobab.

In some of the African villages, the hollow trunk of the giant tree has a doorway rudely cut into it; and is thus made into a vast room, in which the chiefs and principal people of the tribe can meet to discuss matters of business.

The baobab, vast as it is in circumference, does not grow to any great height. It seldom grows higher than sixty feet. It bears a quantity of fruit; each fruit hangs from a long stalk, and is the size and shape of a cucumber.

The monkeys love the fruit, and devour it greedily. This is why the tree has been called the monkey-bread tree.

XXIX

AFRICAN SUN-BIRDS.

THE Cape of Good Hope and the southern parts of Africa are the favourite abode of many gem-like birds that adorn the groves and gardens.

Here they find every sweet they can desire. The rare plants seen in our hot-houses, and the rich exotic flowers that we admire so much, have most of them been brought from Africa.

Turn where we will, in those favoured spots some flower or blossom meets our gaze.

Here are all the families of lilies, painted with the gayest colours, and countless as the sand upon the sea-shore.

Mingling with them is the grotesque orchis, with its bee or bird-like flower, and which covers the meadows, and reaches even to the foot of the mountains. Geraniums of every size and colour grow like weeds, and roses are in the same profusion.

Many of the plants and shrubs yield a sweet and sugary juice. The very gum of the branches is sweet, and in some species can be used as sugar-candy. The natives break it off and eat it.

The Sun-Bird is very fond of a tree called by the natives the sugar-tree, because at the bottom of the flowers it is sure to find a quantity of sugary juice. People gather the flowers of the sugar-tree, and boil down the juice, and use it, as we do sugar, for preserving fruit.

Numbers of little Sun-Birds are always to be seen perched upon the flowers, sipping honey, or making havoc among the insects who, like themselves, are fond of sugar.

And in less fertile spots—even in the waste places with which Africa abounds—many curious plants contrive to exist. One of these plants has great fleshy stems, and flowers that look a little like a star-fish. The smell of the flowers is by no means fragrant. It resembles the odour of decaying meat; and on that account the flower is called " the carrion-flower."

Here, too, growing everywhere, is the fig-marigold, with its bright-coloured petals, and its roots that can not only hold fast to the shifting sand, but draw nourishment from it.

But amid the profusion of flowers, none are more numerous than the heaths. Like the marigolds, they grow everywhere, and they will clothe the barest and most barren rock with beauty.

The flowers of the heath vary in shape as they do in colour. They are cup-shaped, or bell-shaped, or trumpet-shaped; and they are red, and green, and yellow, and purple—every tint, in fact, but blue.

Round the larger flowers are usually swarms of birds and insects. Here are butterflies richly clad, buzzing hosts of bees, and, more beautiful than all, the tiny Sun-Bird, scarcely larger than the butterfly, and which comes to perch on the edge of some velvet petal.

There is a little Sun-Bird, with blue bands glossed with violet, called the Blue-banded Sun-Bird, and which flies in small flocks of eight or ten together. And there is another, the Violet-banded Sun-Bird, still more tiny. And another still, with tufts on either side of brilliant scarlet. Then there is another, called the Fine-backed Sun-Bird. Its head and neck are of a glowing purple, with a bronze-like lustre. The upper parts of the bird are coloured like the petals of the auricula, with a constantly changing lustre. There are no tufts, but on each wing is a patch of the richest violet.

Another beautiful bird has a patch of emerald-green upon its throat; and the fore-parts of the neck and breast are of the brightest scarlet, changing into purple.

This gay plumage disappears when the mating season is over, and the bird becomes of a dull brown, tinted with yellow.

Then there is the Amethyst-throated Sun-Bird, the plumage of which is thick and soft as velvet. On the throat is an oval patch of rich purple, and the wing-feathers are of the same beautiful tint.

It is one of the largest species of the Sun-Birds; and though the velvety feathers are darker than usual, yet the patches of colour make it equal in beauty to any of its tribe.

I might mention, too, the Red-breasted Sun-Bird, a wonderful little creature, with a collar of red and yellow, and the head and neck of a. golden-green. And the Long-tailed Sun-Bird, with a collar of blue; and which is found in Nubia, nestling among the leaves of the acacia-trees.

But the descriptions I could give you, or even pictures themselves, would fail to impart any adequate idea of these gems of Nature—these beautiful birds!

XXX.

THE SPLENDID SUN-BIRD.

————◆————

THE mighty forests of Eastern Africa are nourished and fed by an annual supply of rain. And streams and rivers water the earth. But other parts of the continent are not so favoured. There are tracts of country which suffer from long-continued droughts, and at certain times are barren and waste. The soil is a kind of loose sand, almost like the desert. And yet these tracts of country cannot be called deserts. In spite of the want of rain, and the sandy soil, they will often be covered with plants and shrubs, and grass will clothe the ground, and here and there trees will grow.

Nature has provided a number of plants suited to these arid spots, and able to draw nourishment and subsist where other plants would die. And not only so, but the plants and shrubs found in these parched places can afford a sort of refreshment and comfort to man. The thirsty traveller, making his way over the plain, often comes on a little plant with a stem no thicker than a quill. If he is aware of the nature of the plant, he will rejoice as though he had found a benefactor. He will dig round it, and will presently unearth the root, which is a large round tuber, the size of an infant's head. When he takes off the rind of the tuber, there is a quantity of juicy pulp within, which is cool and refreshing, and suffices to allay his thirst.

There is another creeping plant allied to this, and which bears many tubers, some of them as large as a man's head.

The tubers grow in a circle a little distance from the stem. The natives are very quick at finding out the exact spot where the tuber lies hidden. They strike the ground with a stone, and listen to the sound it makes. Their ears are so sharp they can detect the slightest difference in the sound of the blow. When the tuber is just beneath, the noise of the blow is not the same. And then, in that exact spot, the native begins to dig, and soon finds the treasure he is seeking. Each tuber affords a grateful supply of nourishment and of moisture.

Another refreshing plant of the desert, is the water-melon. Now and then, an unusual quantity of rain will fall and gladden the parched soil. Then the water-melons push forth in abundance, and literally stud the ground. The traveller and his party, and his cattle, may live upon them many days, and care little about any other kind of beverage.

I might mention many more of these water-yielding plants. On the western coast, on the banks of a river that is very often dried up and empty, the hillocks of sand are enriched by a bountiful gourd that grows upon them. It is about the size of a turnip, and has an orange-coloured pulp, the taste of which is very agreeable.

One part of the year, the gourd, or *naras*, as it is called, serves as the staple food of the natives. It contains a number of seeds, a little like almonds, and they dry them in the sun and put them by as a reserve. When the fruit fails, they fall back on the seeds, and are preserved from famine.

This tract of country could not be inhabited but for the naras. Food is scarcely to be obtained, and the natives would perish if they were deprived of this wholesome and agreeable resource.

But there is still another tribe of plants, too curious to be passed over.

To this tribe belongs the fig-marigold, of which we have spoken before, and that is called the Hottentot's fig.

In all other plants, heat and dryness cause the seed-vessels to split open and yield their contents. But it is not so with the marigold. The burning heat and drought keeps the seed-vessels firmly shut. But when rain comes, and the atmosphere is moist and will allow them to grow, the lid opens, and the seeds are shed just at the time when they are certain to vegetate.

One of the marigolds has a tuberous root, which is eaten raw; and from the leaves of another the Hottentots prepare a substance which they chew like tobacco.

In the western part of Africa is found one of the most beautiful of the Sun-Birds. It is called the Splendid Sun-Bird; and no more suitable name could be given to it. Its neck is of a golden-green, and varies in colour with every changing light. Its head and throat sometimes look black, and sometimes of a rich violet. It has a band of scarlet across its breast, and its tail is jet-black, edged with golden-green.

And so do the tints of this wonderful bird change with every light, that the breast looks as if it were banded with blue, and green, and violet. The reason of this play of colours is owing to the structure of the feathers. Each feather has a tip of vermilion, so fine that it is lost against the tint of the feather beneath, and only comes now and then to sight. The base of the feather is a metallic blue or green.

Two lemon-coloured tufts spring from each side

of the breast. This gorgeous bird, thus sumptu-
ously arrayed, visits the great fish-river and the
country round, inhabited by savage tribes. Its
favourite resort is the worm-eaten trunks of the
mimosa-trees, where it makes its nest.

XXXI

THE PLAINS OF AFRICA.

THE great plains of Africa are not only studded with moisture-yielding plants; they are also the abode of all manner of living creatures.

As in the Tropical forest, so it is here,—birds, animals, and insects live in freedom and rove about undisturbed. Here we find the zebra, that no man can tame. Herds of zebras gallop and whirl about in the ample space afforded them. But even here they are timid and watchful, and always suspecting danger. When the zebra is attacked it fights desperately with its hoofs, and often gets the better of its enemy. It has one great enemy; for on these wild plains, the leopard prowls about seeking for prey. Man will sometimes capture the zebra, and try to make it a beast of burden. If it is taken very young, such a thing has been possible; but, except in rare instances, the zebra will rather die than be a captive.

On this expansive plain many objects of interest present themselves. Here are all the different kinds of antelopes.

Yonder little creature, like a goat, is the smallest of the race. It is called the spring-bok, or springing-goat. Its long shining hair is of a beautiful cinnamon colour, while the lower part of the body is a snowy-white.

The horns spread backwards in a curve, and then bend inwards at the points.

The spring-bok has two folds of skin, in the middle of its back, that reach to the tail. When the creature is at rest the folds are not seen, and appear of the same colour as the back. But if it is excited, and begins to take its marvellous leaps, the folds expand, and show a broad patch of the purest white. These springing-antelopes herd together in countless numbers on the plains, and keep as far as possible from the haunts of man. But now and then, in seasons of great drought, the pools dry up, and there is not a drop of water for them to drink.

Then the whole herd makes a descent on the cultivated spots, in numbers so vast that nothing can withstand them.

This is an event the African farmer dreads more than anything that can happen to him. The antelopes come like a swarm of locusts, and any attempt to keep them from the fields is useless. They whiten the country as far as eye can reach; and pastures, which in the morning were fair and flourishing, are trodden down level with the ground.

The farmer is obliged to find fresh fodder for his flocks until such time as the rain comes, when the spring-boks return to their native wilds.

The bounds which the spring-bok can take into the air fill us with astonishment. It will curve its back, showing the white mark, and leap eight feet into the air. It will spring across a path twenty-five feet in width, and clear it at one bound.

The farmer in that part of the world has, in some small degree, his revenge on the antelopes. He kills a great many of them with his gun; for the flesh is as good as venison, and the skin is useful to him for clothing and a variety of purposes. When the rain comes, the great plain that looked like a desert changes its appearance. It blooms like a garden; all kinds of flowers and heaths burst forth in a sheet of colour.

Clouds of brilliant Sun-Birds come to feast upon the nectar they contain, and the butterflies and radiant insects of the Tropics flutter about and enjoy their little day.

Sometimes a black object will appear in the horizon, that gets larger and larger, and at length darkens the sky. The locusts are come; and they fall upon the verdant plain as if resolved to destroy every green blade.

The birds in their turn attack the locusts, and pursue them on the wing, and drive them from place to place. While the scourge of locusts lasts, however man may suffer, the feathered tribes have a continual banquet.

XXXII

THE NAMAQUA SUN-BIRD.

HAVE not quite finished with this part of Africa.

Many wild tribes live scattered about on the plains, obtaining a livelihood from the animals or the plants, or even the insects and the reptiles that abound.

There is the Bushman, who inhabits the most desolate spots, and is so degraded as to be hardly human. He lives by hunting, and follows his prey from place to place.

But he is neither strong nor brave, so that he has recourse to cunning. He uses a poisoned arrow, and is very adroit in aiming it. The poison is so powerful that the animal dies almost at once. Then the Bushman takes out the poisoned part, and generally devours the prey before he quits the spot.

There are some animals whose skin resists the poison; such as the elephant. Then the Bushman makes a pitfall, and covers it with twigs and leaves. Or he goes out some moonlight night armed with his spear, that has a long blade attached to it. One wound alone would have little effect on the elephant, and he could march off with the spear in his body. But the Bushman gives him no rest. He returns to the attack again and again, choosing the moment when the elephant is out of breath, and has just made a furious charge. By degrees, the huge animal gets weak from loss of blood, and falls a victim to the perseverance of his enemy.

Nothing in the way of food comes amiss to the Bushman. He searches out the nest of the Ostrich, and takes the eggs.

When this is done, he hides himself, and waits patiently until the monstrous bird comes home. He shoots it with one of his deadly arrows—

arrows that make such havoc with the wild
creatures of the plain.

But the Bushman cannot always procure sufficient food, even though he will devour snakes,
ants, and locusts.

The women go about collecting roots and
melons, and all the fruits they can find, to eke
out a scanty living.

The Bushman has a neighbour far more provi-
dent than himself. He has just the same diffi-
culties to contend with, for he cannot always procure food; and if it comes a dry season, the melons
and gourds will fail him. But he cultivates a
little garden of his own, and grows herbs and
vegetables for his use. And he has a flock of
goats, which he contrives to keep alive in spite
of the occasional want of water.

Water is as scarce as possible during the long
droughts; and the Bechuana, as he is called, dare
not let his well be seen. His fierce neighbours
would come and rob him of the precious store;
so he is obliged to act with the utmost caution.

He keeps the well covered over with sand, so

that no one can find it; and he lives a long way off. When he is obliged to send for water, a number of women set off and journey to the place. They have bags filled with egg-shells of the Ostrich, which are the only water-vessels they use. They do not open the well, but each woman inserts a reed into it, plunging it in as deep as it will go. Then she draws up the water with her mouth, and puts it out into the egg-shell by her side, filling shell after shell, until she has enough.

The water thus slowly procured is carried home, and every drop is as precious as gold.

When Dr. Livingstone was in this same country, he saw an instance of the great value in which water is held, and that seems scarcely credible to us in this land of streams and rills.

He saw the natives slowly and painfully digging into the dry bed of the river, in hopes of obtaining a few drops of water, that might be drained out of the soil. The drought had been so severe that the grass crumbled to powder when touched; and even insects could not live on the heated and dried surface of the ground.

Among the wild tribes scattered over this part
of Africa a beautiful Sun-Bird is found.

It inhabits the country of the Namaquas, and
is called the Namaqua Sun-Bird.

It has been seen nowhere else, and remains in
this one locality all the year round.

The plumage it wears is grave compared with
many of its family. But a tuft of vivid orange
springs from either side of the breast, and gives it
a beautiful appearance.

The young birds are of a reddish-brown; but
some of them have two pale yellow spots, one
on either side. From these spots by-and-by will
spring the tufts of orange that are so great an
ornament.

· You must not suppose that the Namaquas are
so degraded a race as the Bushmen. They have
herds of cattle, and are far more civilized. But,
like the rest of the African tribes, they are very
cunning, and not at all to be trusted.

XXXIII

THE MALACHITE SUN-BIRD.

THERE is a Sun-Bird which is the largest of the whole species. It is called the Malachite Sun-Bird, and differs a little from its relations. Two of the tail-feathers are of some length, reaching beyond the others for three or more inches.

All the upper parts of the body of this beautiful bird are of a deep green, like malachite, with a changing tint of gold and bronze. The feathers on the head and throat are thick and close, like a pile of velvet, and a little resemble the plumage of the Birds of Paradise. On the breast and neck the colours seem as if waved, the tips

11

of the feathers being green, and the base a deep black. The wings of this splendid bird are black, edged with the same malachite-green, and from the under part are two tufts of brilliant yellow.

It would be scarcely possible to describe the varied tints and hues and changing colours that play every moment over the surface of the plumage. But, after the period of rearing its young has passed, the beautiful Sun-Bird changes its costume. Its radiant tints vanish, and it becomes of a dull green and yellow. Thus it remains, divested of its charms, until the next season arrives. Then the long tail-feathers appear, and the plumage assumes its brilliancy. It again flashes and sparkles, and delights the eye with its wonderful beauty.

The home of the Malachite Sun-Bird is in the southern part of Africa, near the Cape of Good Hope.

Here, in the gardens occupied by the colonists, and in pleasant fertile spots, grow the flowers in which the Sun-Birds delight.

All kinds of acacia-trees bloom in full beauty.

Here is the delicate sensitive-plant that shrinks at a touch; and the tamarind-tree with its graceful foliage and yellow sweet-smelling flowers, and which has stored up, in its pods, a soft acid pulp pleasant to the taste.

And growing nearer to the interior of the continent, farther north than the colony, is the curious butter-tree, so much prized by the natives.

It grows in the thickest part of the forest, and is tall and straight, and with a bark that resembles the ash. The branches spring from the tree at a great height; and when the nuts are ripe they are gathered by the black man as one of his richest treasures.

He prepares them by boiling until the oil or butter is expressed; and in this state it is perfectly white, like our English butter when newly-churned. The native uses it in his cookery as we do butter. And he has another object in preparing it, and quite as important. His toilette could not be made without it. He anoints his skin with the product of the "fat-tree," as he calls it, to prevent the cracks or scabs which are apt to spoil his personal appearance.

Indeed, the "fat-tree" is so precious to him, that if any dearth of the nuts takes place, it is as bad as a famine.

Yet, like the rest of the uncivilized world, he will not be at the pains to cultivate it.

A lady, who was travelling in Africa, made every attempt to see this wonderful tree. It was not possible to reach it, so deep and dense was the forest. But she witnessed the manner in which the butter was prepared; and she brought home a jar filled with it, and it kept sweet and fresh to the end of the journey.

She declared that in frosty, biting weather, nothing that she had ever applied was more healing to the skin.

XXXIV

SUN-BIRDS IN JAVA.

E have visited the far-off land of New Guinea, and the smaller group of the Aru Islands, in search of beautiful birds.

Belonging to the same archipelago of islands . are others of equal interest, and in which we shall find some of the radiant creatures that form the subject of our volume.

In the island of Java there live various species of Sun-Birds that must not be passed over.

One is called the "dark-breasted" Sun-Bird, because of the patch of dark steel blue underneath the throat and breast. On the forehead is

another patch of steel blue; and there is a band
of purple round part of the neck.

Another beautiful bird has a crown of golden
green on the upper part of its head; and its
breast and the lower part of its body are of a rich
crimson purple.   On either side are tufts of
brilliant blue.

The bird is a tiny creature, scarcely four inches
long, and is supposed to live nowhere but in Java.

Java is essentially a forest country.   It is
clothed with dense and mighty forests, that,
except in certain portions, reach from the sea-
shore to the summit of the highest mountains.

The mountains are, nearly all of them, volcanoes; and Java contains more volcanoes, for its
size, than any other tract of country in the world.

These volcanic mountains are formed of the
ashes, and lava, and mud, which from time to time
have been thrown up from the different craters,
and have by degrees accumulated.   Indeed, the
whole island seems to owe its existence to this
cause; and its richness and fertility make it one of
the gardens of the Eastern world.

The open spaces between the forests are like so many parks laid out by the hand of Nature.

Clumps of trees dot the surface of the ground, and give a delightful effect to the scenery.

Here the peacock struts about, as well as in the forest glades; and as evening approaches. its harsh scream begins to be heard. Then the native hastens to his dwelling, perhaps in one of the villages that are scattered here and there in wild and lonely places. He shuts himself in, and is glad to find himself in security. It is a popular belief that, when the peacock is heard, the tiger issues forth for his night's depredations. Nothing is more dangerous than to venture along the park-like plains, inviting as they seem, without a plentiful supply of fire-arms. Often, before any-thing is seen, the horses stand still and tremble violently. The tiger may lurk only a few yards distant, hidden by some patch of jungle, and be ready to take his fatal spring.

He is a handsome creature, with stripes of black and gold, and every movement is full of grace. But he is the scourge of this beautiful island; and scarce a native family, in these tiger-haunted places, but has had some member of it carried away and devoured.

Java abounds in all the riches of the tropical world : birds and insects wear the splendid colours that belong to the land of perpetual summer.

The insects attain a size beyond what is ever known in England. There are gigantic spiders, that spin a network so strong that it has to be cut with a knife.

On one of these powerful threads the spider suspends itself, as in mid-air, across the forest glade, and seems mounted on some aërial bridge. The birds might seize on the tempting morsel displayed thus openly before them. But Nature has protected the spider by giving it a number of sharp spines that stick out of its body. Some of these spines are longer than the body of the spider itself, and render it an unpleasant morsel for a bird to swallow.

In England, the spider wears a very sombre dress ; but in the Tropics it is far otherwise. The spider is arrayed in as rich a costume as the Sun-Bird or the Humming-Bird.

It has stripes of yellow, black, orange, and green ; and marks and characters of the most grotesque description are painted on its body.

These brilliantly-marked spiders live among the flowers and foliage. Those of the species that lurk in gloomy places, wear a dark and sombre attire, as if in unison with their habits.

One spider with a black body and scarlet sides, lives on the seeds of a tree which are marked in exactly the same manner as itself.

The spiders have many enemies ; for they are not all protected by spines. In Java there is a kind of sparrow that lives almost entirely on spiders, and is named from this very habit. The bird has a long slender bill curved backwards ; and it can search for the spider, and drag it from the most secure hiding-place.

There is a curious sight often met with in Java.

The traveller who approaches a village may happen to see a tree covered with black objects, which he supposes to be the fruit.

The objects, however, turn out to be nothing of the kind. He soon perceives a disagreeable scent, and hears a piping noise. The black objects resolve themselves into a troop of bats!

There they hang, head downwards, from the branches to which they have hooked themselves, waiting for the dusk of evening, when they will fly forth in search of prey.

The largest bat in the world lives in Java.

XXXV

SUN-BIRD IN SUMATRA.

OME fifteen miles from Java lies the great island of Sumatra. Here we are close under the Equator, for the imaginary line runs obliquely through the island. A beautiful Sun-Bird flits about, under the fierce rays of the vertical sun, and makes its home here. It has a blue patch on the forehead, and a stripe of the same colour on the sides of the neck. The upper part of the back is a dark red, and the breast is also red, but of a lighter shade. The tail feathers are blue.

This bird, which is one of the tiny gems in the family of Sun-Birds, was mentioned by Sir Stam-

ford Raffles, in a list he made of the birds of Java
and Sumatra.   He was once governor of these
islands, and to him we are indebted for many discoveries in natural history.

It was he who first came upon the monstrous
flower called after himself "the Rafflesia," and
which was growing unknown and unheard of in
the forests of Sumatra.

It belongs to a class of plants much akin
to the *fungi*, and is a parasite in its habits.
It has neither root nor leaves; but the flower,
huge as it is, and the largest flower in the world,
issues from the root or stem of a tree, and
gradually opens its flesh-like petals.   The odour it
gives out is anything but agreeable, and resembles
decaying meat.

Here, too, is the curious leaf-like butterfly that
so deceives the naturalist.   He sees it flying about
with its bright colours, and a band of deep
orange across its wings.   Then, all at once, it is
gone, and seems as if it had vanished by magic.
He searches for it in vain; and though he can
point out the exact spot where he saw it last, he

cannot find it. But all the time it is close by him, and he has looked at it again and again without recognizing it.

It has settled on a twig, with its wings closed, and looks so much like a leaf that he has mistaken it for one. The reason of this great resemblance is soon explained. The upper wings of the butterfly end in a fine point like the tip of a leaf, and the lower wings end in a projection very much like a stalk; and, besides that, there is a stripe up the wing that looks exactly like the midrib of the leaf, and there are other markings that correspond with the veins.

The butterfly drops down upon a twig, and is thus lost sight of; and this is the way it escapes many of its enemies.

The Sun-Bird in the Picture was named after Mrs. Gould, the wife of Mr. Gould the naturalist. It wears, as you see, a costume of blue, yellow, and red, and has light brown wings which are always in motion. As it flutters in the sunlight, it seems some fairy creature decked in gold and azure and all the tints of the rainbow.

XXXVI

THE FIERY-TAILED SUN-BIRD.

HERE is a country that, in olden time, was looked upon as a kind of magic region.

The travellers who made their way thither, brought home wonderful accounts of the products of the place. But gradually the fairy region became more trodden and better known. In these days, every part of India is familiar.

It reaches from the ranges of the Himalaya Mountains to the point of Cape Comorin; and though the fables once believed have passed away, it is well known to abound in the rarest and the richest productions.

India is the home of almost every beautiful bird, insect, and flower, that exists within the range of the Tropics; and the scenery in many parts may well be compared to fairy-land.

Here grow the trees and plants which are of such service to man, and the products of which are borne in merchant-vessels to every part of the globe. The cotton, the rice, the arrow-root, the indigo, all kinds of dyes, and spices, and fabrics of the finest texture, almost as fine as gossamer, come from India. And here are pearls, and ivory, and gold, and gems—indeed, the riches of the world seem poured out in this favoured land.

The fertility of India is occasioned by the plentiful supply of moisture yielded to it. The mountain ranges, which look down on the plains of India, have their summits covered with snow. The melting of the snow forms the source of number-less streams, and of the great rivers that gladden the land. Thus supplied with heat and moisture, herbs, trees, and flowers flourish with the utmost luxuriance.

Beautiful birds surround us on every hand.

Each fairy bower and forest glade abounds with them.

When the morning sun shines on the crown of the palm trees, a cloud of Parrots, like streaks or patches of vivid colour, fly forth in search of a stream in which to take their early bath. Humming-Birds, of radiant hues, sparkle among the branches, and gorgeous Fly-catchers pursue the insects that flutter on every side.

Here we find the Sun-Birds like tiny gems perching on the flowers, or climbing among the branches. In the Picture, you see the Fiery-tailed, or, as he is sometimes called, the Red-tailed Sun-Bird.

He is a native of a part of India called Silhet, a province which borders on Bengal, and has a capital town of the same name.

You see in what glowing costume he is clad. The upper part of the head and the throat are blue, changing into violet. Then comes a patch, or mark, of orange scarlet. The wings are purple, edged with green, while the breast is yellow.

The fiery tail is, as you perceive, of the same

orange scarlet; and two of the tail feathers reach to a considerable distance.

Amid the wealth of flowers, and under the burning sun in which he delights, the Sun-Bird enjoys his little day. The trees of the forest are crowned with fragrant flowers, on which he loves to perch; or he visits the gardens, rich with tropical beauty. His tiny nest is composed of the finest down, picked, perhaps, from the cotton tree, and mixed with dead leaves.

A resident in India watched the little Sun-Birds build their nest.

They began by fixing some materials to the great web of a spider, that hung from a twig. The materials consisted of fragments of paper, threads of cloth, grass, and other substances; and when the nest was finished it hung suspended from the web, like a little ball in the air.

THE NEPAUL SUN-BIRD.

THERE is in India an extensive plain enclosed between ranges of mountains, and called the territory of Nepaul. It resembles a kind of amphitheatre, covered with towns and villages. It is so surrounded by hills and mountains, that it cannot be entered or quitted without passing by one or other of them.

The northern part of the territory enjoys a temperate climate, such as Europe; for snow lies upon the tops of the mountain, and will even sprinkle the valley. Hoar-frost will be known and heard of in these localities; but the rivers

are never frozen, nor is there any great severity
of climate.

For some distance up the mountain sides, you
find yourself in all the rich vegetation of the Tropics. Nay, in the deep sheltered valleys, which
wind into the heart of the mountains, the same
brilliant flora prevails. Here are palms and
acacias, here are trees clothed with the grotesque
orchis, and here are the feathery tufts of the
bamboo.

Higher still, are oaks and forest trees of a more
northern growth, and even the pine.

The musk-deer is a source of wealth to the
inhabitants of Nepaul. They hunt it for the sake
of the musk that it secretes, and that is so much
prized as a perfume.

The deer leads a solitary life, in the wild rocky
places on the borders of the snow. It has no
horns or antlers, and differs in other respects from
the stag or the antelope.

In winter it comes down to more temperate
spots, and this is the only time when the hunter
has a chance of capturing it. Even then his task

is a very difficult one. He sets a snare, or else goes out with his bow and arrow. But the creature is so shy, that he is often obliged to imitate the cry of the young one, in order to induce the old deer to approach within reach of his arrows.

The difficulty of obtaining the musk causes it to be sold at a very high price; and hunting the deer would be a profitable employment, were they more easy to capture.

The musk is sent to England, and comes in little bags or sacks. It is well known in the toilette, and to many people the scent is agreeable.

It is also used as a medicine.

In the forests that clothe the mountains of Nepaul is found a lovely Sun-Bird.

Its bill and legs are of a wood-brown; the top of the head a golden-green, changing into purple; and the neck and back a deep carmine-red. The cheeks, throat, and breast of this beautiful bird are of a dazzling scarlet. The lower part of the body has a band or mark of pale yellow; but when the bird is at rest, the long feathers of the tail conceal this yellow band.

This exquisite little gem is by no means rare in the dense forests of which we have spoken. It finds in the thick foliage an abundance of spiders, ants, and other insects, on which it feeds, and is seen flitting among the deep recesses like a sunbeam.

There is another beautiful bird in this locality, called the Nepaul Sun-Bird. The head, throat, and neck are blue, and there is a crescent-shaped band of chestnut on the breast. The under parts of the body are yellow, and the middle of the breast is of bright orange. I might tell you of still another Sun-Bird found here; but only one specimen has reached us, and that had been greatly injured.

On the sides of the neck are two stripes, or, as they are called, moustaches, of a rich blue, changing into violet and pink. The tail feathers are of the same rich colours; and they are broad at the base, and loose from each other, so that the bird can spread them out like a fan. The under part of the body is black.

XXXVIII

THE CEYLON SUN-BIRD.

MONG the lovely groves and gardens of Ceylon sports the dainty little Sun-Bird in the Picture.

It is dressed, as you perceive, in the gay attire of the beautiful birds. Its throat is a rich purple mixed with black, and the body is a glowing yellow; while the band across the throat, and the tail feathers, are a deep brown.

Nothing can exceed the beauty of this tiny gem, as it perches itself on the petal of some tropical flower, and feeds upon its juices, picking off, as it does so, the insects which have found a home there. Its note is quick and sharp and impatient, and it

passes from blossom to blossom with great rapidity.
The honeyed nectar of flowers is its favourite food,
and when in captivity it will sip sugar and water
with delight.

It builds a nest a little in the shape of a bottle
with a long neck, and suspends it from the extreme branch of a tree. The nest is made of the
very fine fibres of plants, and has a round hole on
one side, through which the bird can enter.

The brilliant Sun-Birds, with their purple and
yellow costumes, are found not only in Ceylon,
but also in India. The gardens and groves
abound with them, and the tiny nest is constantly seen hanging from the branches of the
trees.

The mother Sun-Bird wears a grave and sober
attire. The upper part of her body is a plain
olive-green, and her throat is white. The colours
of her wings and tail resemble those of her mate.

There is a family of birds allied to the Sun-
Birds, and very much like them. They live upon
the nectar of flowers, and are called Honey-eaters.

The beak is long and curved like the Sun-Bird's,

and the tongue is divided into two slender filaments. Their costume is not so gay as that of the
Sun-Bird's, but there are two or three bright yellow feathers on each wing.

These feathers are highly esteemed by the
natives of the South Sea Islands, where the
Honey-Eater makes its home.

The chiefs wear them on their royal mantles
and robes of state. The robes are ample and flowing, and are completely covered with feathers.

The head-dresses, worn by the ladies of rank,
are also made of the same yellow feathers, and
are considered of almost priceless value.

Another species of the Honey-eater has scarlet
feathers, and these are also used. The idols of the
natives are often adorned with them.

XXXIX

THE HUMMING-BIRD.

————◆————

HE Humming-Bird is a relation of the Sun-Bird, but is rather different in his habits; for he hovers over the flower, and sucks the juices, without settling upon it. Poised in the air, he peeps cautiously, with his sparkling eye, into the recesses of the flower, vibrating his wings so rapidly that you can hardly see them. All the time, he makes a low, humming sound, that is very pleasant to listen to, and that seems to lull the insects within the flower to sleep. Then out darts his long delicate tongue, and takes them up, one after the other; and he finishes as the Sun-Bird did, by sipping a little honey.

The Humming-Bird is as fond of insects as he is of honey, and besides catching them on the wing, he has been seen to steal them out of the spiders' webs. This is rather dangerous work, for if his wings were to be entangled he would be taken prisoner, and then woe betide him! He has a wholesome dread of the great spider I have told you about, and if he only shows himself, off the Humming-Bird darts like a sun-beam; for the spider is as large as he is, and a great deal fiercer. But he can rob the smaller spiders with less danger; and he picks out the insects from their webs, snatching them away in a hurry, and then darting off, to come back again the next minute; and so on, until the spider is left with an empty larder.

All the strength of the Humming-Bird lies in his wings, that are large in proportion to his tiny body. They are a little like those of the Swift in shape, and everybody knows how rapidly the Swift can dart about, and cleave the air with his pinions. The feathers, on the quills of the Humming-Bird's wing, are so firmly united that they are almost like a thin plate of whalebone. No air can pass through them, and this is why they make a humming sound, as the bird vibrates his wings.

The Humming-Bird needs these strong wings to support himself in the air, as his feet are too weak and delicate to perch for any length of time.

And he depends very much upon his wings for safety.

There will come the season of rain and storm, and his little nest will be beaten down, and his home among the trees and flowers be made a wreck. Before this happens, he must fly many long miles to get from beneath the clouds. He looks too fairy-like to undertake such a journey; but his wings are powerful enough to bear him out of reach of danger. They will transport him to other lands, where the storm has passed, and the trees and flowers are blooming as gaily as ever.

The long bill of the Humming-Bird has been given him that he may search to the bottom of the large tubular flowers, and rifle their sweet juices. But some of these flowers are so bent that a straight bill would not be able to reach the honey ; so the bird that feeds upon them has his bill curved upwards at the tip, that he may follow the bend of the flower, and not be disappointed of his feast.

The tongue is not unlike the tongue of the Woodpecker, and is darted out in the same way, and for the same purpose, of entrapping insects.

It is composed of two tubes, joined together nearly the whole of their length, and ending in a spoon-like point. It is very sticky, so the insects when touched by it cannot escape ; and it is also fringed with minute spines or bristles, that still further help to secure the prey.

The forest, with its great trees covered with climbing-plants and flowers, swarms with these brilliant little creatures.

> " Like fairy sprites, a thousand birds
> Glance by on golden wing ;
> Birds lovelier than the lovely hues
> Of the bloom wherein they sing."

No wonder the ancient Mexicans stole the plumage of the Humming-Birds to adorn their mantles; and very superb these mantles were, sparkling with many-coloured tints. And the Mexican youth thought he could make no more costly present to his bride than the gorgeous crest of the Humming-Bird, to be worn amongst her hair. Even now, the Indian women hang the tiny bodies of the Humming-Birds to their ears, instead of earrings; and on their head-dresses, instead of jewels.

The Humming-Bird, though so small, is very brave, and will attack a bird three or four times his own size. It is no pleasant thing to come in the way of his long bill, for he always pecks at the eyes of his assailant.

When he is keeping watch over the nest he is particularly fierce, and if another bird happen to come near, he darts out, screaming with rage ; his throat swells, and his wings expand to their fullest extent, and he looks like a little fury. He gives battle to the intruder, and the two birds fight desperately, until one of them falls to the ground exhausted, and so ends the conflict.

I am afraid the Humming-Bird is a very passionate little fellow. He will even go into a rage with a flower that does not please him, or has not

so much honey in it as he expected; and then he
tears it to pieces, and scatters it with his bill and
claws.

Perhaps the best part of his character comes
out when he is helping his little partner to build
their nest. He brings her all the materials, and
flies about collecting them with the greatest in-
dustry. The tiny nest is generally hung to the
end of a twig of the orange or pomegranate tree,
and is completely hidden by one of the large
leaves, that overhangs it, and forms a canopy.
The nest is sometimes made entirely of thistle-
down; and the prickly burs of the thistle are
stuck outside to protect it. But moss and cotton
are used quite as often, and dead leaves woven in
among them.

The cotton grows upon a tree called the silk-
cotton tree, that is a native of these tropical
countries. It is a very large tree indeed, and
is looked upon by the black people with great
veneration. They never venture to throw a stone
at it; and when they are obliged to cut it down
they pour some wine at its root, in order to pre-

vent its being angry, and doing them any harm! It is one of the few trees that shed their leaves; for a tropical forest is always green and full of foliage, as the new leaves come out before the old ones drop.

But, every other year, the silk-cotton tree stands quite bare, and without a single leaf; and then its trunk and great branches are dotted all over with seed-pods. As soon as the pods are ripe they burst, and out comes a quantity of fine silky down, that is carried away by the wind. It cannot be used as cotton, for it will not twist or hold together, and all that can be done with it is to stuff pillows and mattresses. But, as it floats hither and thither, it is a rich harvest for the little Humming-Birds. Hundreds of them may be seen darting about, pursuing the tufts of down, and carrying them away in their bills. When the nest is made, the mother bird lays two eggs in it, no bigger than peas, and of a snow-white colour, speckled here and there with yellow.

She and her mate sit upon the nest by turns, and never leave it a moment. At the end of twelve days, the two little Humming-Birds come out of their shells, and are about the size of blue-bottle flies. At first they are unfledged, but very soon are covered with down ; and in time, feathers grow upon them, and become as beautiful as those of the parent birds.

XL

THE HUMMING-BIRDS OF THE FOREST.

HE beautiful birds we are now describing are divided into families or groups.

There is one tribe of Humming-Birds that have their home in the shade of the forest. They obtain their food from leaves, since but few flowers are met with in these secluded and shady places. They search for insects on the vast tropical foliage of the trees, threading their way about with great dexterity, and picking off the insects that swarm above and beneath.

The Humming-Birds of the forest are very numerous. Their nests are made of the fibres of plants, and dry mosses and lichens, closely woven together. They are often lined with the beautiful silk-cotton of which I have spoken, and that provides such abundant materials for the birds. The nest is long, and shaped like a purse. There is a Humming-Bird, in South America, that leads almost the life of a moth or a bat. It has two long tail-feathers that cross each other; and its dress is red and gold and green, and changes colour every moment.

It chooses the woods by the side of rivers, and dark and lonely places. Very early in the morning, the bird comes out of its retreat in search of insects. But no sooner does the sun appear, and his flaming rays light up the sky, than the Humming-Bird disappears. It dislikes the glare and heat of the tropical day, and hides in its cool retreat until the evening. Then it comes out again, and darts hither and thither in search of its prey. But for its brilliant colours, you might take it for a bird of night.

The nest is built on a twig that overhangs some lonely creek. It is very much like a piece of tanned leather, and has a kind of ridge or rim round the top.

This rim is to prevent the eggs from rolling out.

The range of the Humming-Birds, like that of the Parrots, is wider than was once imagined.

The tropical region is their natural home ; and every attempt to rear them in our colder climate has been in vain.

But they have been known to wander far beyond the limits of the Torrid Zone. They pay flying visits to Canada, and even travel as far as the land of the Seal and the Penguin. In the Southern Hemisphere, Humming-Birds have been seen in Patagonia. But this seems to have been a mere summer excursion, for they retreated before the first breath of autumn.

XLI

PHAON COMET HUMMING-BIRD.

HERE is a part of South America which is, next to Thibet, the highest country in the world. It is a kind of plateau situated between two ranges of the Andes, and is very much larger than England. Indeed, it would take nine such islands as England to make one tract of country like Bolivia.

I have brought you here, because in Bolivia, and also in Peru, there are some of the beautiful birds we are describing.

In the Picture, you see a creature of rare and exquisite loveliness. It is called the Phaon Comet, and indeed it flashes, and sparkles, and

HUMMING BIRDS

The Phaon Comet & Chimborazian Hill Star

glitters like one of those glowing and wandering meteors above.

Nothing can be more gorgeous than its attire. The feathers of the back are a deep luminous crimson, its throat is like an emerald, and the magnificent tail-feathers are barred with black.

It has all the habits of its race, and perhaps a larger share of courage and of swiftness. It sweeps through the air, like the spear with which the Indian struck at the Cockatoo, and its whirling headlong movements remind us of the weapon. Sometimes the eye is wearied with these ceaseless evolutions, and then the bird will drop, like a falling star, into some huge blossom, and be hidden from sight.

In the high table-land of Bolivia the cold is intense, and the icy winds sweep over with chilling breath. The soil is barren and unfruitful, and we look in vain for the birds and flowers of the Tropics. But the deep sheltered valleys are fertile in the extreme, and produce sugar, cotton, and all the riches of a sunny clime.

The table-land, cold and rugged as it is, has

many inhabitants; for here are found those wonderful mines of gold and silver that were such a
source of wealth to the Spaniards. And here a
city was built, called Potosi, which is the most
elevated city in the world.

The mountain on which the city stands is
pierced in every direction by the shafts of mines.
At night, when the mines were working, and used
to glow with the light of innumerable furnaces,
the sight was very grand indeed.

At one time, more than fifteen thousand persons
were employed at the mines. But the veins of
ore are now less productive, and are comparatively
deserted.

You may imagine the desolate state of the
country round Potosi; nothing is to be seen but
bare rocks, covered with moss. The mountains
are tipped with perpetual snow.

The poor Indian would fare badly enough, but
for certain plants, which are given by Nature for
his comfort. There is a plant which grows at a
great height above the sea, and in places where
no other seed or grain could ripen. It is called

quinoa, and the seeds can be prepared in many
different ways. The leaves can also be made into
a kind of beer.

But the greatest consolation to the Indian is
another plant called *coca,* which is abundant in
the sheltered valleys. It thrives in these tropical
spots, and also on the heights, and is as carefully
cultivated and as important as the crop of corn is
with us.

The plantations of coca are seen on the steep
sides of the valleys, rising to an amazing height
above the level of the sea. The plant is about the
size of our English blackthorn, and has a shining
green foliage and small white flowers, which ripen
into scarlet berries.

The berries are not used, but the leaves are
gathered and dried in the sun. They are chewed
by the Indian with great delight, and he is never
seen without his leathern pouch full of coca, and
which also contains a little box of powdered lime.

His manner of chewing is to work up the morsel
of coca into a ball, then, taking it from his mouth,
he plunges a piece of wood like a tooth-pick into

the lime, and pierces the ball through and through with it until it gets the taste of lime. That is just how he likes it.

But one ball will not content him, and he goes on chewing until he is often in a state of intoxication. Thus a valuable plant is made a source of evil. But the Indian would not give up his coca on any terms whatever : he stops his work three times a day in order to chew it, and it serves him almost in the stead of food.

XLII

THE HILL-STAR HUMMING-BIRD.

NE of the luxuriant valleys situated among the Andes is called the Valley of Quito. Here is the capital city of a portion of South America named Quito, a province that includes hill and dale, rock and mountain, and all kinds of temperatures and productions. The climate of the valley is delicious. Here seems to reign an ever verdant spring. No extremes of heat or cold reach this favoured spot.

It is clothed with fruitful fields and orchards, and flocks and herds, and populous villages. It looks to the traveller the abode of beauty and content. But the most dangerous volcanoes in the world hem in the lovely valley of Quito.

Smoke and flame are often seen issuing from their snow-clad tops. The snow will suddenly melt before some violent eruption, and floods will desolate the happy valley.

The flames of Cotopaxi, the most famous of the volcanoes, have been known to rise three thousand feet above the top of the mountain, and its frightful roar is heard a hundred and fifty miles distant!

Nothing can be more dangerous than the neighbourhood of these volcanoes. Under ground are stores of hidden fire, and elements of mischief that break out with violence.

The inhabitants are always in danger of earthquakes. Then the scene baffles description. The earth reels and groans, trees are torn up by the roots, and rocks are rent into fragments. Blue flames issue from the ground, and people and houses, flocks and herds, are involved in destruction.

The natives. of Quito may be said to live in perpetual hazard. But they do not seem to realize the fact. They are a gay, light-hearted race, fond of pleasure, and of revelling in all the delights of their beautiful country. For here, as if to atone for other drawbacks, the fruits of the earth ripen with wonderful rapidity. Sowing and reaping are carried on at once.

There is a mighty peak of the Andes, said by some to be the highest peak in the world. It is not a volcano, but its sides are thickly covered with snow, and though in the midst of the Tropics, the temperature in the neighbourhood is intensely cold.

Yet I have brought you here to behold the spot where a Humming-Bird chooses to dwell!

You see him in the Picture. He has his name from the mountain, and is called the Chimborazian Hill-Star.

A star of beauty indeed he is! His costume is magnificent. The head and throat are violet, and there is a ring of shining green round the neck. The white of the under part of his body contrasts with the brilliant colours that adorn him. His bill is black as jet.

This star-like creature haunts the grand mountain of Chimborazo, and ascends nearly to the line where snow commences.

Here grows the gray lichen, the last of the plants, lingering on the verge of eternal snow. Lower down are stunted bushes and meadows of saxifrage; and then comes the wax-palm, its leaves coated with a substance like wax.

Lower still is the grotesque orchis, the pineapple, the fern, the laurel, and the fragrant myrtle.

As you descend, the colours deepen in richness, and the climate becomes more and more tropical, until, at length, you find yourself among the rich foliage and gorgeous flowers of the Torrid Zone. Thus a succession of pictures are presented by the hand of Nature.

The Humming-Bird feeds on the Alpine plants, and makes his nest of moss and lichen, and fastens it under the ledge of a rock. Here the mother-bird lays two tiny eggs, from which the young Humming-Birds will issue.

XLIII

THE RUBY-THROATED HUMMING-BIRD.

N the early spring, when the warm sun brings out countless flowers and blossoms, the inhabitants of the United States, and other portions of North America, are rejoiced to behold a fairy creature, light as air, and with resplendent colours, advance to the gardens and groves. Its gorgeous throat glows with fiery red ; the feathers are very strong, and lie upon each other like scales. As the bird moves they change from crimson to black, and from black to crimson.

Its costume of lustrous green changes and sparkles like the light of emeralds. Its movements are as the lightning flash, or the glow of a sunbeam. It darts from flower to flower like a gleam of light, visiting orchard and prairie and grove.

The whole land, with its mighty forests, vast meadows, and majestic rivers, is as one garden of delight. The bird is recognized and admired everywhere.

"The Ruby-throated Humming-Bird is come!"

Many a long stretch of country, over hill, dale, river, and forest, have the wings of the bird borne it in safety. It is provided with no weapons of defence. It owes its safety to its rapid flight, its courage, and its minute size, which screens it from observation.

Now it appears in full beauty, and prepared to sport through the long summer hours with ever new delight!

It has its favourites amongst the flowers. Do you see that brilliant sheet of scarlet? That is the trumpet-flower, which the Humming-Bird loves.

It comes to the blossom, and poises over it a

few seconds. Its wings are like a mist, and are almost invisible as they vibrate in the air. But you can catch sight of the ruby throat, and the golden green of the back.

Presently the bill is thrust into the flower, and picks out an insect. Then the bird retires to some withered twig, on which it perches to arrange its plumage. Its note is like the chirp of the grasshopper, and is now and then uttered as it flits from flower to flower, or when it is engaged in battle with one of its companions.

The Humming-Bird is very brave. It will attack a bird double its own size; even the tyrant Fly-catcher is often driven away, and pursued for a short distance.

Now and then the great humble-bee comes droning by, and makes an attack on the radiant creature in its path. But there is little danger from such a clumsy foe. The Humming-Bird darts away, and is out of sight in a moment.

Its own flight is like that of the bee, only far more rapid. It darts in at the open window of a room, attracted by the scent of some fragrant bouquet. It gives the flowers a passing notice, and is gone ere you can well behold it.

When the season grows late, and the evenings are cool, the Humming-Bird can find many places of refuge.

It enters the hothouse or conservatory, and uses it for a sleeping-room; going thence in the morning, and returning at night. When the season gets later still, the Humming-Bird disappears altogether.

Cold is very dreadful to this child of the Tropics. Sun and heat are necessary to its existence. If deprived of them it dies.

A Humming-Bird was once put into a cage, and placed in a shady room. The weather was cool, and the poor little bird, after fluttering about for a time, fell down as if stupified. It lay with its eyes closed, and giving no signs of life. The owner of the bird carried it out of doors, and placed it in the sun.

Quickly a change was observed. The bird began to breathe more freely; its eyes opened, and even sparkled with their usual brilliancy.

When it had quite recovered, no further effort was made to detain it, and it flew joyfully to the top of a tree, and, perching on a branch, began to dress its plumage.

The rays of the sun had restored the bird to life.

The nest of the Ruby-throated Humming-Bird is the most delicate fabric that ever was seen. The outside is made of the same gray old lichen that coats over the branch where the tiny nest is fixed. The bird works with such skill that it contrives to make the nest look as if it were part of the branch. The atoms of lichen that it uses are gummed together with saliva. The next coating is of some silky down it has picked up; and the innermost lining of all is of the softest fibres of plants, that make a silken couch for the eggs to lie upon.

XLIV

THE HUMMING-BIRD OF NOOTKA SOUND.

———◆———

N the western coast of North America, as far north as the Temperate Zone, is a bay, or, as it is called, a *sound*. The entrance lies between two rocky points, and when these are cleared, the bay widens out and contains a number of islands of different extent.

Many years ago, Captain Cook entered this sound, and was the first to discover its existence. He anchored his ship near to one of the larger islands, and gave the bay the name of Nootka Sound, which it has retained ever since.

The climate here is very mild,—much milder

than on the opposite coast of America, in precisely the same latitude.

Here were woods of the lime, and cypress, and other trees; and though the gorgeous flowers we have spoken of were not to be seen, yet others of a humbler form and colour sprinkled the earth. Strawberries, raspberries, and currants grew in abundance; and the butter-cup, the wild-rose, and many of our English weeds, were in full bloom.

Squirrels were at play among the branches of the trees; and there were a few species of birds, such as Eagles, Woodpeckers, Kingfishers; and on the coast there were Swans, and Gulls, and Wild-Ducks.

But a discovery was made in this sequestered spot by Captain Cook. He saw one of the beautiful birds of which we are speaking. It is called the Ruff-necked Humming-Bird, or the "Humming-Bird of Nootka Sound."

In one of his excursions on the island, he came upon a number of brilliant birds, glowing with the rich colours of their tribe, and flashing from flower to flower, or poising over them with the habit peculiar to their race.

As he approached a bush, out darted a radiant creature, like a flame of fire, and passed close by him, as though it would attack his face, returning again and again to the charge, and whirling about in the utmost fury.

This was the male bird, on the watch to drive away any intruder from the nest. The angry, hissing noise it made, was like that of a ball as it whizzes through the air.

A few days after, Captain Cook found the nest on the forked branch of a bramble. The mother-bird was sitting on her eggs. She flew out, and hovered near him while he examined the nest. But when he went away, she took her place again, and continued to sit on her eggs as before. The nest was as tiny and light as possible. It was made of lichen and moss, and a few feathers woven together with the slender rootlets of plants, and was lined with thistle-down.

The plumage of the bird is soft and beautifully blended, and glossed like velvet. The upper parts are a rich orange, and the head a bronzed green and purple. The feathers of the throat and the sides of the neck are a magnificent fiery red, with a tint of yellow or green, according to the light in which you see them. On the lower part of the neck is a band of reddish-white.

On a clear day, the bird may be seen rising high in the air, and then descending, to mount again. While it descends, it utters a curious note, which resembles the noise made by the branches of a tree as they rub together in a high wind.

This singular note would hardly be supposed to proceed from a bird, still less from the tiny creature that produces it. If the weather is dull or cloudy, the Humming-Bird is silent.

The mother-bird wears a different costume to that of her mate. She is clad in golden-green; and instead of the orange throat, she has spots of a glowing ruby.

In this remote and inhospitable spot, where we should least expect to find them, do we thus come upon the beautiful birds!

XLV

THE MANGO HUMMING-BIRD.

HERE is one species of Humming-Bird that is more hardy than the rest of its tribe, and has been brought to England.

It is called the Mango Humming-Bird, and is very common in the parts of the world where it lives. The Mango Humming-Birds are seen everywhere.

They are beautiful birds, as you will judge from the description I am about to give you.

Under the throat and body is a deep rich stripe of velvety black, shaded with the brilliant blue which so often makes part of the costume of the Humming-Bird.

The upper part of the body is the usual golden-green. The tail-feathers are rounded at the tip, and are violet or purple, according to the light in which you see them.

A female Humming-Bird was once sitting in her nest, when a young man who was passing saw her. He contrived to cut off the branch with the nest and the bird together, and to bring them away. A few days after, he sailed for England, and during the passage he fed the bird with honey and water. She grew very tame, and continued to hatch her eggs, out of which came, in course of time, two tiny creatures no bigger than blue-bottle flies.

These little Humming-Birds began to grow and thrive. But the mother did not long survive her imprisonment. She very soon died, and the young birds were left to the care of their owner.

He contrived to keep them alive for some few weeks after they reached England, in spite of the coolness of the climate. One of the tiny gems was petted by a lady, who allowed it to sip honey from her lips.

The home of the Mango Humming-Bird is in the West Indies, and in the flowery land of Florida.

Parts of this beautiful country abound with flowers; so much so, that its name has been given to it on this very account. Orange and lemon trees grow wild in the utmost abundance, and their blossoms afford a delicious banquet to the birds. Cotton is produced in great plenty in this tropical clime; and the rich dye called indigo is brought from here.

The indigo-plant is a child of the sun, and cannot thrive anywhere but in the Tropics. Indeed, it requires a certain temperature to enable it to vegetate.

It is a shrub-like plant, rising about two feet from the ground, and its leaves a little resemble those of the acacia. When it begins to flower, the owner of the plantation cuts it down with a sickle; and then it will sprout again, and bear a second crop. In this genial clime, the planter will sometimes obtain four crops a year.

In the mighty forests of this part of the world,

where the trunks and branches of the trees are clothed with brilliant parasites and spikes of flowers of every hue, the Humming - Birds are met with by thousands.

And in the gardens and cultivated places they are equally abundant; and so devoid of fear, that a bird will hover over a blossom while the owner is plucking another from the same bush !

The mango itself is one of the beneficent trees of the Tropics. It has great spreading branches; and the foliage is so dense that a fugitive may hide amidst it, and be rarely found by his pursuers, though they are searching the very tree.

The taste of the fruit is sweet and luscious, and in the season the black people live almost entirely upon it. The cattle also are fed, and even fattened, upon mangoes. In Jamaica, a basket of mangoes may be had for the trouble of climbing the tree and shaking the branches.

XLVI.

GOULD'S COQUETTE.

———‡———

HERE is a naturalist we have spoken of before, who has spent much time and labour in studying the habits of the Humming - Bird. He has given us a great deal of information about them, in a book written for the purpose, and which is the most valuable we have on the subject.

The lovely bird in the Picture is named after him, "Gould's Humming-Bird," or "Gould's Coquette."

It is one of the most beautiful of its tribe. Its head and crest are of vivid red; its wings are

purple; and it wears on its neck a frill of long
white feathers tipped with golden-green.

There is a strong likeness said to exist between the Humming-Birds and some of the
insect tribe. The Humming-Bird seems more
allied to the moth or the butterfly than to the rest
of the birds. There is one moth so much like it,
that the naturalist has been known to shoot it by
mistake for the tiny gem we have been describing.
It is called the "humming-bird hawk-moth." It
is rather smaller than the Humming-Bird, but
has just the same habits. It darts and whirls
about with wonderful quickness, and hovers over
the flower just as the bird does.

It has a long trunk or proboscis, which it thrusts
into the flower in search of food. At the end of
its body is a tuft or brush, which, when spread
open, is not unlike the tail of a bird.

The natives of Brazil seem much struck with
the likeness we are speaking of. They believe that
the moth turns into the bird, and that the bird was
first a moth. They tried to impress their fancy on
a naturalist who was visiting that part of the world.

"Look," they said to him; "their heads are the same, and so are their tails."

The naturalist found it impossible to argue them out of this belief.

Even an English gentleman once stoutly maintained that he had seen a Humming-Bird in England. For one species of the hawk-moth is found in our own country; and you may see it whirling and hovering and darting about in our gardens. The gentleman had seen the moth, and had mistaken it for a Humming-Bird.

The orange-groves, in those sunny lands where the Humming-Birds live, are covered all the year round with blossom. But at certain seasons their beauty reaches perfection. They are a mass of fruit and blossom.

Then come the beautiful birds in flocks, sparkling and shining and glistening in the sun like gold and gems.

They whirl about the trees, darting so swiftly that you can scarcely see them. When they pause, it is but for a moment. Down goes the bill, and the bird is off again, darting from blossom to blossom, not in a regular manner, but at random, and as by caprice.

Sometimes two Humming-Birds come to the same flower. Then they quarrel violently, and mount upwards, doing fierce battle with each other. But the storm soon passes over, and the birds dart off again in search of insects. Their movements are so rapid that the eye cannot catch the brilliant colours that adorn them. Nor can one species be distinguished from another, unless there happens to be a conspicuous patch of white, mixed with the lovely tints of their plumage.

I should tell you that the female Humming-Bird does not wear the brilliant colours of her mate. She is dressed in a more sober costume, and is therefore not so much prized.

XLVII

THE MARVELLOUS HUMMING-BIRD.

——◆◆——

THE Marvellous Humming-Bird has perhaps no equal in beauty in the world.
It is a creature that floats about on wings
of azure and emerald. It wears a crown
of brilliant blue, and a collar of green encircles the
throat. The sides of the breast are a soft white;
and the wonderful tail-feathers—that project to a
great length—are tipped with brown.

This rare creature was first discovered in Peru,
—a country of both desert and of verdure, of rich
tropical spots and of burning sand.

This curious region, which presents such different aspects, lies on the sea-coast, between the

great mountains of the Cordilleras and the Pacific Ocean.

Rain seldom falls here ; and the green spots are caused by some rill or stream that descends from the mountains. The inhabitants prize every drop of the precious stream, and use it to water their fields and gardens. At the line where the artificial system of irrigation ends, the desert again begins.

On these spots, thus won from the sand, all the rich verdure of the Tropics is seen. Here is cotton, and sugar, and maize, and the products of a burning clime. And here are beautiful birds of every shade and hue. Here is the Parrot, and the Pigeon, and the Crowned Fly-catcher, dressed in a costume of fiery red.

In this strange land, mist supplies the place of rain. At a certain season of the year there comes a veil over the sky, and a kind of ceaseless drizzle takes place.

The drizzle, unpleasant as it must be, falls on the barren places and dry arid plains with all the blessing of dew or of rain. They become green and fertile, and the whole land rejoices.

Myriads of sea-birds are found on the shore. And on some islands close by, successive generations have made their home for centuries.

As no rain falls, the droppings of the birds have been accumulating for ages, and would remain undisturbed, if man had not found out their value. His ships go constantly to fetch away the bird-manure, or guano, as it is called. It is of the greatest benefit to the farmer, and used by him to enrich his land. Not a mine of gold or silver could be more important.

XLVIII

THE HUMMING-BIRD OF ROBINSON CRUSOE'S ISLAND.

———✦———

SOME long time ago, a Spanish sailor used to steer his vessel backwards and forwards between Peru and Chili.

He was always baffled by contrary winds, and it occurred to him that if he stood out farther to sea he might escape them.

He put this idea in practice; and during his next voyage, when at sea, he fell in with an island hitherto undiscovered. From a distance, the island looked like a mass of rocks and mountains, and had a barren appearance. But as he approached, the prospect improved; the mountains were clothed with trees, and there were fertile valleys, watered by crystal streams. And here and there, a cascade bounded from rock to rock, and glided along like a thread of silver.

All kinds of tropical plants and trees grew on the sheltered parts of the island. Here were palm-trees, and the cotton, and the pepper. And here were myrtle-trees of great size, so that the trunks could be sawed into planks forty feet long.

A tall grass, as high as a man, covered these fertile spots, and looked like a crop of oats. And there were ferns, and creepers, and clover, and many other familiar plants. The island had no human inhabitants; but birds and insects were met with. Here were great spiders, that wove gigantic webs from tree to tree. And here were the Albatross and the Hawk; and a bird that made a hole in the ground, like a rabbit, and fed upon fish. Every night, this bird used to utter a note like the words "Be quiet!"

And here were Humming-Birds in all their brilliant beauty. Perhaps the most beautiful Humming-Bird ever seen is found in this remote spot.   It was discovered, not many years ago, by Captain King, and its name added to the list of Humming-Birds that were known to live in the island.

The blue crown of the bird is composed of scaly feathers, which spread out to some length, and form a crest of surpassing beauty.

The upper part of the body is a bright emerald-green, and the two middle feathers of the tail are green ; the others, green outside and a clear white beneath.   The cheeks of this wonderful bird are a purple-green, with pink or violet spots, according to the light.   The under part of the body is pure white, with round spots of the richest golden-green, that contrast with the snowy ground on which they are marked.

Nothing can exceed the splendour of this magnificent bird.   Indeed, every description falls short of the reality.   It is as if Nature in this remote spot excelled herself.   The name by which the brilliant gem is known is "Stokes's Humming-Bird."

The Spanish sailor gave his own name to the

island, and called it Juan Fernandez. He was allowed to possess the newly-discovered spot, and even made an attempt to colonize it. But the few families who went to settle there did not remain. They soon abandoned it, and it was uninhabited as before.

Juan Fernandez is known to every reader of "Robinson Crusoe," as the island on which he and his man Friday lived in solitude.

The real solitary, or exile, was a seaman of the name of Alexander Selkirk, who quitted his vessel, and was left behind in this desolate place. He spent four years without hearing the sound of a human voice ; and was at last picked up and brought to England. The goats, in whose skins he had clothed himself, were the descendants of those animals brought by the colonists I have mentioned, and that had multiplied and overrun the island.

XLIX

THE AZURE CROWN HUMMING-BIRD.

———•———

N the tropical regions of Brazil, the birds have no need to migrate, from one part of the country to another, to escape the winter. There is no cold season to drive them from their haunts and homes. So that the Cuckoo never flits, as she does in England, and the Swallow is seen making his aërial curves and sweeps the whole year round.

But many reasons impel the birds at times to wander.

At one season of the year, great rains fall and deluge the ground. Then, the forest becomes too damp and cool to be pleasant to the birds.

And more than that, in the open country an abundant banquet is awaiting them. The trees are loaded with the most tempting fruit. Here are ripe oranges, hanging in profusion, their golden hue displaying itself amid the flowers and blossoms of the tree.

Here is the banana, and many more bending under their rich burden. The maize-fields and the rice-fields are equally tempting; and such a lure cannot be resisted.

Forth come the birds, from the damp gloomy forest, to the fields, and groves, and uplands.

Each bird makes for its especial food. The Parrots fall upon the fields of maize. The Toucans devour the bananas with keen relish. And the Finch tribe, clad in costume of blue and scarlet, make for the rice.

Many beautiful birds, rarely seen at other times, are now abroad, flaunting their rich plumage in the open fields.

The Indian hunter, and the white man who has settled in the country, takes, the one his rifle, and the other his blow-pipe and his poisoned arrow.

The white man can shoot numbers of beautiful birds without much trouble. The gay Cotinga, the Parrot, and the Toucan, fall alike beneath his gun.

The Indian is on the watch for a splendid Macaw, that is generally out of his reach in the recesses of the forest.

But the magnificent bird, with its flaming colours, has ventured from its retreat, to banquet on certain fruits in which it delights, and which grow in the open country. The Indian shoots as many Macaws as he can. He has an eye for colour, and he uses their feathers to plume his arrows, and to adorn his person.

In these bird-hunting expeditions, the Indian is more patient and hardy than the white man. He continues his watch for days with the utmost vigilance. And his quick ear and eye can detect sounds and signals, when his more civilized neighbour would be at fault.

This rich and varied country has its share of Humming-Birds.

Among the beautiful birds that shine and glisten, they take their place. The perpetual summer, the gorgeous flowers, the abundance of insects, render bird-life a continual banquet.

The Golden-green Humming-Bird is met with, here, and is one of the smallest, but most exquisite of the tribe.

The tiny creature wears, as its name indicates, a costume of golden-green with an ever-changing lustre.   The wings are a brownish-purple, and the tail an indigo-blue.

Then there is the bird in the Picture, which is called the Azure Crown, — a bird of rare and enchanting beauty.

It is larger than the tiny gem just mentioned. The bill is a clear yellow with a black tip, and the under parts of the body a pure white.

On the back of the head is a hood or cowl of glittering blue, which is the " azure crown."

HUMMING BIRDS

The Golden Tail and the Azure Crown

L

GOLDEN TAIL.

———◆———

HE beautiful birds that abound in Brazil, as in all tropical countries, furnish a rich material for the native toilette— such a material as we in these colder climes cannot boast of. The ancient tribes of the country adorned themselves with the plumage of the birds, and nowhere could they obtain more rich variety. The Macaw, the Trogon, the Cotinga — almost all the birds we have named—yield plumes and feathers of wondrous beauty.

And the feather-flowers, made by the Indians, are esteemed the loveliest ornaments by people of civilized countries; and have made their way to Europe.

Now and then, a splendid bouquet is purchased by the European, that is not altogether what it professes. The leaves should be made of the feathers of the Parrot; but instead of this, the Indian has procured plumes from the back of some other bird more easily met with—such as the White Ibis—and dyed them to imitate the gaudy tints of the Parrot.

The Scarlet Ibis and the Rose-coloured Spoonbill, both of which are found on the shores of the mighty rivers that run through the forest, yield the most gay-coloured feathers.

The carnation, or the tulip, or even the queen of the flowers, the rose, is imitated with the most exquisite skill, and makes an ornament of rare beauty for the tresses of an Indian belle.

There is a certain tribe of Indians, living on the banks of one of the rivers, that wear a head-dress of the most gorgeous colours.

It is a coronet of red and yellow feathers, firmly plaited together, and fitted to a fillet or band, encircling the head. These feathers are not of their natural colour. They belong to some of the transformed Parrots of which I have spoken, and are very highly prized. Nothing but actual necessity will induce an Indian to part with his head-dress.

The ladies of Brazil imitate this fashion of wearing the feathers of birds. They love to adorn themselves with flowers, made of the bright-coloured plumage that so delights the Indian.

And not one of the flowers, thus artificially produced, can vie with those made from the breasts and the throats of the Humming-Birds. These exquisite ornaments can hardly be described. In the bonnet, or amid the hair, they flash and sparkle with wonderful brilliance. The emerald, the topaz,—all the famous jewels of the East seem to pale before them.

In the Picture, you see one of these gems of Nature, that inhabits the forests of Brazil. It is called the "Golden Tail;" and dazzles the eye with the swiftness of its movements.

The Golden Tail Humming-Bird wears a crown

of rich dark blue, with a tinge of green. Green
and gold adorn the upper surface of the body, and
a golden tint flashes with remarkable brilliance
from the under parts of the wings. The tail
glistens with the richest tint of gold, and the under
surface of the body is a shining green.

This rare creature flits and flashes in the deep
forests and open plains, in the gardens and the
groves of Brazil.

But, besides the beautiful birds, the Indian has
still another resource for his toilette. The insects, in this land of radiant colours, are in their
way as splendid as the birds.

They shine and sparkle like living gold.
The Indian will often make his flowers of the
lustrous wings of a beetle; or, treating the insect
as if it were a precious stone, will have its body
set in gold, like a brooch. And, as if Nature
delighted in every form of radiance, and to flash
and sparkle with increasing lustre before the eye,
here are the whole race of fire-flies—gleaming in
the darkness like so many stars.

The Indian is attracted to them as to the beautiful birds. He captures the living spark, as it glows with its own light, and uses it for a torch to guide him through the forest gloom.

And the ladies place the brilliant spark amid their hair, letting it gleam and sparkle like a diamond; or they wear a robe of gossamer texture, through which glow a myriad of fire-flies, so that the wearer seems as if clad in a starry vesture !

LI

RUFFED AND TUFTED HUMMING-BIRDS.

HAVE not told you half the varieties met with in the costume of the beautiful birds.

There is an ornament worn by a Humming-Bird that lives in the forests of Brazil. This bird has two thick tufts of deep indigo blue, springing from under the eyes and forming a kind of ruff. Each tuft is tipped with yellow, which contrasts with the intense blue of the breast. On the forehead the feathers look like scales, and are of a bright green. And there is a band of deep velvety black running in a line from eye to eye. The throat and part of the neck are of a shining green;

and here are long narrow feathers, that form a collar or breastplate of green against the blue.

The tail-feathers are broad and expanded, and of a metallic green. It is difficult to imagine such a rare and sumptuous creature, even in this land of beauty.

There is a Humming-Bird, also in Brazil, called the Tufted-necked Humming-Bird. It wears a large crest of clear chestnut, and the sides of the neck are adorned with tufts of narrow feathers. The tufts or plumes are of the same colour as the crest, and end in a tip of shining green. The throat and the upper part of the breast, and also the forehead, are covered with scale-like feathers of a brilliant green. The back is of a bronzed green shaded with blue, and separated from the tail-feathers by a band or stripe of white.

The tail is broad, and spreads out in a fan-like shape ; and is green and chestnut, with shades of purple.

These exquisite little birds with the tufts and ruffs I have just described, are called by the French "Coquettes." This is a playful idea suggested by the ornament worn by the bird.   It can set up its beautiful ruff, and give itself the most attractive appearance.

For it is during the courting season that the ruff appears in its full beauty.

The bird in the Picture has a ruff of the most fairy-like description.   And it has a crest of chestnut and green, while the throat is yellow. It is one of the family of Coquettes, and lives in Peru.

Thousands of Humming-Birds, rare to us, but common enough in these sunny lands, sport in the forests of Brazil, and are clad in rainbow vesture.

The traveller beholds them as in a vast aviary, flashing brightness and beauty on every side.

Here are a whole bevy of beautiful birds. Crowds of Parrots sidle about on the branches, or dress their gaudy plumage ; and here are the caressing Love-Birds, and the flaming Macaws. And close by, sits the solemn Trogon in his resplendent plumes.   And little gleams of blue and scarlet among the branches show the presence of innumerable Cotingas, as brisk and gay as possible.

Beneath, on the moist earth, are numbers of living creatures. Here are lizards, and snakes, and insects of every kind. Here is the armadillo, that rustles among the decaying leaves; and the curious ant-eater, with its long tongue and its clog-like feet. And a deer will now and then bound through some leafy opening, pursued by the jaguar. And the tapir, with its swine-like snout, will come crashing by.

Up above, in the topmost tier of branches, where giant trees push their crowns into light and air, is a vast leafy region, all matted and bound together by the ropes and cables of the forest.

On this mighty plateau the monkeys live in security, and run nimbly about, and grin and chatter and frolic. Not even the thunder and lightning of the white man's gun can reach them. And the squirrel bounds from bough to bough, with wild delight.

Standing as we do, in this magical spot, surrounded with all the wonders of the Tropics, a peculiar sound meets our ear.

There comes up from the distance a clear shrill whistle, like the well-known signal of a railway train.   Such a thing cannot be, in this remote spot.   But, as sure as morning, noon, and evening come, it is heard.

A grasshopper makes this curious utterance. Not more curious than another sound, like a hammer, that marks the hours, through the tropical night, with the utmost regularity.

This watchman of the night is a frog, called by the natives the " Hammersmith."

And in the scorching noon, weary and parched with thirst, the traveller is sometimes mocked by a small brown bird, that repeats in his ears the tantalizing words that mean, in the language of the country, " Have you no water ? "

LII

THE CRIMSON TOPAZ.

HE part of the world in which the lovely bird in the Picture is found, is rich in many interesting scenes and valuable productions.

It is called Guiana, and is a territory to the north of South America.

Here again the tropical forest presents every variety of wonder. The most curious object met with, in its wild recesses, is a tree called the mora, which towers aloft, its topmost branches often white and bare with age. A fig-tree that has the habits of a parasite chooses the mora to subsist upon.

The fig-tree is about the size of our English

apple-tree, and it shoots forth from one of the thick branches of the mora, near to the top.

When the figs are ripe, they yield a rich harvest to the birds. Crowds of birds flock round them; and to this very circumstance the fig-tree owed its existence.

A bird dropped the seed of the fig-tree on the branch of the mora. It had been feasting on some neighbouring figs, and had perched on the mora to digest its banquet.

Up to this time the mora was flourishing in all its luxuriance. But the seed dropped by the bird sent out its rootlets into the branches, and began to draw nourishment from the sap.

The sap caused it to grow with vigour, and mount upwards. But when it became a fig-tree yielding fruit, it also, though a parasite, became the abode of other parasites. The birds, as they flocked to it, dropped seeds that began to grow upon its branches, as its own seed had grown upon the mora-tree. Thus parasite after parasite took hold on each other, and all were maintained by the sap and juices of the mora!

But the tree, thus encumbered, cannot long support its burdens. After a time, it will languish and decay. And then the whole brood of parasites, cut off from their supplies, will perish with it. Often, in the forest, the traveller stands to gaze on a tree so covered with parasites that not a vestige of the trunk or the branches can be seen.

Some of these parasites bear flowers of brilliant beauty, that seem to start, as by magic, from the branch or stem on which they grow.

And others have a strange and almost mournful aspect, as they hang from the tree like ragged tufts of hair.

They are known by the name of the "monkey's beard," or the "old man's beard."

The thick black filaments of the plant are like horse-hair, and are used by the natives as such, to stuff their cushions and mattresses.

The birds find in this curious parasite a material ever at hand, of which they can build their nests.

There is a little bird dressed in black and orange, and that is called the Baltimore. It picks up a long thread of the "beard" and fixes it by either end to a branch. This is the beginning of the nest. Then comes the other bird with another thread, and fixes it side by side with the first.

Thus the two birds assist each other in building the nest; and it is woven so firmly that no tempest and no rain can injure it.

The nest of the Crimson Topaz is made of a fungus, and fastened together with a fine net like a cobweb. It is of the shape of a cup, and is found in some sheltered spot, or dark and lonely creek.

The bird itself sparkles like a jewel, and well deserves its name of Topaz. Its colours are gorgeous; and the feathers seem to overlap each other like scales.

Nothing can be more splendid than the tail-feathers of this beautiful bird. They are, as you see, orange and green, and the throat is the loveliest green and yellow.

The Crimson Topaz is the largest of the Humming-Birds. The mother-bird lays two eggs in her cup-like nest.

LIII

THE PURPLE-CRESTED HUMMING-BIRD.

———

HE territory of Guiana abounds in many kinds of Humming-Birds. There is the Black-crested Humming-Bird, with a breastplate of emerald-green, while the centre of the breast is black ; and the White-tailed Humming-Bird, with a tail of white, except the middle feathers, which are green.

And there is the Humming-Bird in the Picture, with the upper part of the body a purplish-black, and the wings of an olive-green. The bright grass-green of the tail is very striking. This beautiful bird is called the Purple-crested Humming-Bird, and is to be seen in the West Indian Islands, as well as in Guiana.

The forests of Guiana swarm with birds of every hue and tint. Crowds of little creatures, some of them no bigger than a Wren, but clad in brilliant colours, fly about in troops, to seek for insects on the leaves and branches of the trees. These are the Manakins. They have a low sweet note, uttered from time to time as they hop about.

Then there is a bird like the Mocking-Bird, dressed in black and yellow, that makes all kinds of curious noises. Whatever bird happens to be singing, it will mimic him, and sing almost as well. So that there appears to be a succession of birds. Now you hear the cry of the Toucan, now the hammering of the Woodpecker. If even a dog bark, the sound will be mimicked!

In the most secluded part of the forest, a bird lives that is so rare that he is scarcely ever seen.

He is called the "Cock of the Rock," and wears a very beautiful costume of orange; and has on his head a great comb or crest, that gives him his name. These birds are said by the Indians to

hold " dancing-parties," after the manner of the
Birds of Paradise.   But, in this case, only one
bird performs; and the rest look on, and clap their
wings by way of applause.

This is the moment chosen by the Indian to
creep cautiously to the spot with his blow-pipe.

The birds are so occupied that they do not perceive his approach, until he has shot several of
them.

LIV

OTHER INHABITANTS OF THE FOREST.

OU must not suppose that the tropical forest is solely occupied by the animal world.

It has other inhabitants, who find a home within its extensive bounds. Here and there, a small portion of it is cleared, and a settler builds a little wooden house, and has a plantation of coffee or of cocoa.

Some of these wooden dwellings are very picturesque, and are covered with roses and jessamine, and shaded with fruit-trees. But the life of the white man, even though surrounded by the luxuriance of Nature, is lonely, and he is rarely happy.

Should he, however, content himself with his lot, he becomes a kind of forest king ; and, like the Indian, gets acquainted with every herb and flower, and every tree and bush, near his little domain. And he knows the voices of the birds, and the animals, and leads a life of perfect freedom, if not of enjoyment.

Besides the settlers in the forest, there are many runaway negroes, who subsist by hunting and by plunder, and are not very pleasant to meet with. And there are different tribes of Indians, who wander about in the accessible parts of the forest.

These wandering tribes are, many of them, low enough in the scale of intelligence. But they are skilled in the forest paths, and the forest lore.

They know the properties of plants, and where to obtain their terrible poisons. And they understand the habits of birds and animals, and can track them with patience and dexterity.

The Indians, in the forests of Guiana, are a

fierce and jealous race. The different tribes hate each other, and never meet except to fight.

They are so suspicious, that when a tribe marches over a sandy district, they tread in each other's steps, and the Indians who are last in the file take care to obliterate all trace of footmarks.

They do this lest another tribe should find out where they are gone, and be upon their track.

In these forests are a tribe of earth-eating Indians. Their huts are stored with round balls, that look like dumplings, and, indeed, form part of the larder. But the dumplings are made of an oily kind of clay that the Indian relishes extremely.

He does not, as was once supposed, eat this strange food from necessity, but from choice. You could not offer him anything more to his taste.

The hut of the Indian is sometimes floored with wood.

There are trees in the forest, strange as it may seem, that cannot be made to burn. The Indian knows which trees they are, and he uses them for the purpose I have mentioned. Fires are constantly made on these wooden floors, but there is no fear of an accident.

The plague of insects in the forest is very great, and, to the white man, intolerable.

There is the fire-ant of Guiana, that inflicts cruel tortures. It is a tiny creature, and would seem incapable of doing much mischief. But the ants live in vast communities, and construct hillocks which the traveller may chance to pass. Then out rush hosts of ants, and innumerable pincers wound his skin, until the pain is almost more than he can bear. It has been compared to the effect of boiling water poured on the legs and feet. There is a venom in the bite of the fire-ant; and the creature is so tenacious, it will be torn in pieces rather than quit its hold.

LV

CORA SHEAR-TAIL HUMMING-BIRD.

EVERY part of the strange country of Peru is hilly, if not mountainous. The valleys are little better than ravines; and the rivers flow with the rushing noise of torrents, and fall in cascades of foam as they make their way to the sea.

A journey in Peru is attended with some difficulty. Along the desert strip of land near to the shore, heat, thirst, and fatigue, to say nothing of the attacks of robbers, are to be feared. But the interior of the country is beset with many dangers and trials worse than these.

Here are precipices of a frightful description,

and glaciers, and avalanches; and, indeed, all the risks and perils of an Alpine country.

Sometimes the valley traversed is barely wide enough to allow the travellers to pass. It might be called a narrow cleft between two perpendicular rocks, that here and there nearly touch each other.

Masses of half-loosened rock threaten to fall from the sides of the precipice every moment. Nay, such a thing often takes place, and mules, and even travellers, will be swept into the abyss.

On these mountains, part of the grand range of the Cordilleras, people are seized with fainting, and a malady like sea-sickness. The height above the level of the sea is ten thousand feet.

Another disease often met with is blindness. The brilliance of the sun on the dazzling white of the snow has that effect; and the utmost caution is necessary to protect the eyes from the excessive glare.

Now and then, the traveller is overtaken by a terrific storm of thunder and lightning. For hours the flashes continue with awful brilliancy, and the white snow looks as if tinged with blood.

The traveller is obliged to abandon his mule, and creep under the shelter of some rock or cave until the storm is over.

And here, too, in his journey over this wild part of the country, he comes upon those wonderful bridges that look like mere threads over an abyss.

The bridge is, in fact, merely a thick strip of hide or undressed leather that is fixed from one side of the torrent to the other.

A couple more strips are fixed over the chasm, and made to serve as a balustrade; and on this frail support the traveller has to venture his life, the bridge swaying with an unsteady motion at every step.

And more dangerous still is another bridge, made of a mere rope stretched from side to side, or bank to bank. A rough kind of chair is fastened to the rope, and in it the traveller seats himself, and is pulled slowly across by another rope attached to the chair, and in the hands of some one on the opposite bank.

The wild table-lands of Peru are called "the uninhabited." But Nature contrives a scanty kind of pasture. In some places are patches of the gentian, a true mountain-flower; and here is the verbena, and the ornament of our English gardens, the calceolaria. And here are a few dwarfed-looking shrubs that the inhabitants of this desolate region use for fuel, or to roof their miserable huts.

And here are some of the animals most valuable to man. The beautiful little chinchilla has a relation here, with warm soft fur that can be used as a garment. And here is the llama and the alpaca, and the tribe of creatures with shining wool that afford us a variety of materials for clothing. And here is the mighty condor, the largest of the birds. He soars to the highest peak of the Andes, and seems to look down on mountain, forest, and river.

But, in reality, his piercing eye is searching for prey, and he will presently swoop on some poor mule that has fallen beneath its burden amid the bleak passes of the rocks.

Even here, wild as the scenery is, there are many beautiful birds.

Here is a species of Goose with snowy plumage and dark-green wings. And here, in the swamps and marshes, is the Scarlet Flamingo; and here is the Ibis, and the Plover, and the Gull.

In the sheltered valleys, the traveller seems to step from the blasts of winter to the joys of perpetual spring. From the wretched hut of the Indian, on the heights yonder, he may, in a few hours, journey to the land of the Humming-Bird and the palm. Here he may feast on tropical fruits, and be surrounded by fields and meadows, rich in all the plenteousness of harvest.

The elevated country near Lima, the capital of Peru, is the home of the beautiful bird in the Picture. It is a tiny creature, and has, as you see, two of its tail-feathers very long indeed.

Many of the Humming-Birds have been named after precious stones; such as the emerald, the topaz, and the ruby, which their flashing plumage resembles. The bird in the Picture has given to it the musical name of Cora,—a name very common among the ladies of Peru.

Years ago, Peru was an independent nation, and governed by the Incas, who were priests as well as princes. The Peruvians worshipped the Sun, and had temples in his honour. And there were maidens who were made priestesses of the Sun, and were occupied in the idolatrous rites of their religion, and in keeping alive the fires and lamps upon the altars.

Cora is the name given to one of these maidens by a French author in a story he has written, and the scene of which is laid in ancient Peru.

The Humming-Bird gets its title of Cora from that story.

LVI

THE GREEN-TAILED SYLPH.

N the tropical world, everything appears to be on a grand scale. The forests, of which we have spoken, clothe an extent of country that seems almost boundless.

Great Britain itself would find ample space within the limits of one of these forests!

And equally vast are the far-stretching plains that occur in some parts of South America, and go by the name of "Llanos."

They reach for more than two hundred thousand miles; and present a level surface which, at certain seasons, is scorched by the rays of the tropical sun.

This is the season when no rain falls, and every living thing is scorched and blasted by the intolerable heat.

But here and there grows a palm, that is the blessing of the desert. While a particle of moisture remains in the ground, it collects round the root of the tree, and makes a little pool of water.

At one time of the year even these pools are dried up.

The palm of which I am speaking is called the Mauritia, or fan-palm, because its leaves spread out in the shape of a fan.

A tribe of Indians who live in these plains, subsist almost entirely on the produce of the fan-palm.

The meal-like substance contained in the stem yields a nutritious article of food, and is made into bread. The cone-shaped fruit is also eaten, and the sap is made into a sweet wine.

At times, when the great river Orinoco overflows its banks, and inundates the dwellings of the Indians, they have recourse to the palm as to a place of refuge.

They climb nimbly up its branches, with the

agility of monkeys.   Here they are often obliged
to remain for some time; and they suspend their
mats in the boughs, and take up their abode
literally with the monkeys.

And a curious sight it is, to those on board
some vessel sailing up the river, to behold the
twinkling of lights in the tree-tops.   The lights
are kindled by the Indians in their aërial dwellings.

Another palm grows in the territory of New
Granada, that is of equal service to man.

Its leaves are very large, and are used to thatch
the native huts.   But it is the nut that yields the
substance to which I refer.

It yields a clear tasteless juice, that is refreshing
as a beverage in that hot climate; but if it is
allowed to remain untouched, it soon becomes
white and milky, and in the end sets hard and
solid, like ivory.

This is the vegetable ivory of which so many
toys and fancy articles are made.   If the vegetable ivory is put in water it will soften; but on
being taken out, it quickly becomes hard again.

It is so like the ivory of the elephant's tusks, that it cannot be distinguished from it.

The beautiful bird in the Picture lives in this part of the world, and frequents the banks of the great rivers.

It belongs to the tribe of Humming-Birds that have tails more or less forked.

The name of Sylph has been given to it perhaps on account of its exceeding grace and loveliness. The colours of its sapphire throat, and emerald crown, and olive-green feathers, blend harmoniously together. Its long forked green tail is tipped with yellow.

To this family group belong many birds with tails deeply forked, and that are of great beauty. There is the Racket-tailed Humming-Bird, that has a spoon-like tip at the end of each fork, a little like the Racquet-tailed Kingfisher; and the Black-capped Humming-Bird, with a black crest, and tail-feathers also black, and lengthened to a considerable extent; and the Swallow-tailed Humming-Bird, with a tail of indigo blue.

LVII.

THE GREAT CRESTED COQUETTE.

HE bird in the Picture, though it comes last in the volume, is by no means least in beauty.

It is one of the loveliest of the beautiful birds.

The shape of its body very much resembles that of the humming-bird hawk-moth, of which we have spoken before.

Its wings are small, and of a purplish-brown colour. The neck and upper part of the body are clothed with green and gold, and the feathers are arranged to look like a gorget. The tail is chestnut-red, and is slightly forked. But the most brilliant ornament worn by the Coquette — for such it is — consists of a splendid orange crest of a shining red, and the feathers of which rise up into a point. Nothing can exceed the beauty of this sparkling crest, as it glitters in the sun. It gives to the bird an appearance that can hardly be described.

The Coquette has even been spoken of as a "winged flame."

In the Picture, it is poising over a flower. Its wings appear motionless, but in reality they beat with such swiftness that the eye cannot catch their movements. The bird utters a cry that sounds like the word " Hour, hour ;" and its bill, like a dagger, is ready to be plunged into the flower the moment it perceives an insect. Now and then the bird has been seen to attack the flower itself, and tear it in pieces, like some beautiful fury.

The home of the Coquette is in the country of Bolivia, and along the banks of the great rivers.

For the rivers in America, like the mountains and the plains, are on a scale of the utmost magnitude.   They wind along with the grandeur almost of the ocean.

The giant river of South America is the Amazon, that in places spreads out into an expanse of water of a pale yellowish orange, and is as much as six miles in breadth.

Trunks of trees, and fruit and leaves, and fragments of the forest, float in vast quantities down the river.   And beds of aquatic plants line the shore.   Masses of these plants, looking like seaweeds, detach themselves, here and there, and form floating islands.

On either bank of the river is the dense and mighty forest, that presents us with a succession of pictures.   Here are stems of different colours, black, red, yellow, and silvery gray.   And here is the feathery palm; and here are festoons and garlands of colour, as the parasitic plants droop from the branches and, in places, touch the water.

The water's edge is alive with birds.   Here are crowds of water-fowl.   Here is the Heron, standing patiently for hours, his eye fixed on the water beneath, in which he hopes presently to spy out a fish. And here is the Scarlet Flamingo, like a soldier sentinel, and the White Ibis, and many more.

Overhead fly the sea-birds, the Gull and the Tern, as though this mighty river were the ocean. The Gulls utter all night their hoarse cry. By day they often amuse themselves by sitting in a row on some floating log of wood in the middle of the stream, and sailing down, as if they enjoyed the voyage.

They deposit their eggs in the sand-banks. And the Indian, who is very observant of the habits of the birds, says, that in the middle of the day they carry drops of water in their bills, to moisten the eggs, and prevent them from being spoiled by the excessive heat.

And here, as in the sea, a shoal of porpoises will tumble clumsily about. And, to the terror of those who are sailing on the water, a grim alligator will swim slowly by.

The waters abound in fish. And here is found a species of salmon, called the "piranga." This

little creature bites terribly, and attacks everything it meets with. The waters will be stained
with the blood of its victim.

A person who chances to bathe or swim in the
neighbourhood of the pirangas is sure to suffer.
He will be lacerated by a number of sharp
teeth, that seem as if they were bent upon devouring him.

The poor stag is now and then actually devoured. When pressed by an enemy, he will
plunge into the water, and attempt to swim across ;
but he will be so bitten and wounded by the
merciless pirangas, that he sinks from exhaustion,
and becomes their prey.

Even the huge alligator has his tail often
wounded by the pirangas. But they themselves
are not without enemies to keep them in check.

The Indian catches many of them, for he thinks
them a delicate article of food.

The river forms a line of division between one
tribe of creatures and another.

The monkeys that live in the forest on one side
of the river differ from the monkeys on the other

side. Thus the river is like a sea that divides territories and races one from the other.

Here are two separate regions teeming with different occupants. And, as if still further to keep up the resemblance to the ocean, the hoarse cry of the Petrel and the Sea-mew is heard; and they dart along the water and skim the waves, as though they mistook them for the briny deep!.